THE TRUTH ABOUT OUTSOURCING

The Truth About Outsourcing

b11693630

Brian Rothery and Ian Robertson

Gower

Published by
Gower Publishing Limited
Gower House
Croft Road
Aldershot
Hampshire GU11 3HR
England

Gower
Old Post Road
Brookfield
Vermont 05036
USA

Reprinted 1996

Brian Rothery and Ian Robertson have asserted their right under the Copyright, Designs and Patents Act 1988 to be identified as the authors of this work.

British Library Cataloguing in Publication Data
Rothery, Brian
    The truth About outsourcing
    I. Title II.   Robertson, Ian
    658.4038011

ISBN 0–566–07515–6

Library of Congress Cataloging-in-Publication Data
Rothery, Brian
    The truth about outsourcing/Brian Rothery and Ian Robertson.
        p.   cm.
    ISBN 0–566–07515–6
    1. Contracting out.   2. Contracting out—Case studies.
    I. Robertson, Ian, 1944–   .   II. Title.
HD3858.R66   1995
658.7'2—dc20

95-42649
CIP

Typeset in 11 point Palatino by Poole Typesetting (Wessex) Ltd, Bournemouth and printed in Great Britain by Hartnolls Ltd, Bodmin.

Contents

List of illustrations

Preface

The term 'outsourcing' is used to describe a phenomenon which is sweeping industry. It is possibly a part of the wider movement of society towards shaping a more productive and less wasteful world. Outsourcing presents management with sensitive human relations challenges as never before, as it can affect any employee and any manager outside the so-called 'core competencies'.

As no structured approach already exists, or may not be readily available, this book provides both a description of the strategy of outsourcing and a methodology for going about it. It is therefore aimed at senior management.

Part I describes the drivers behind the increasing practice of outsourcing, the kinds of work which can be outsourced, the core competencies normally retained, the pitfalls and the nature of the project involved.

Part II examines specific sectors and applications, while the appendices provide useful checklists, including important legal considerations and a proposed methodology.

Brian Rothery
Ian Robertson

Acknowledgements

The authors would like to thank all those who have helped in the preparation of material for this book. In addition to being listed here, full acknowledgements have been made in the relevant sections: Turner Kenneth Brown, Solicitors, and HMSO; Tony Tatton-Brown, BCO; Susan McGarry, Vice President of The Yankee Group; Input Corporation; Technology Forecaster, Inc.; the Body Shop and the Lane Group; John Gillett of IBM; Rachel Burnett, Partner with the Computer and Communications Group, Masons, Solicitors.

BR
IR

PART I
THE OUTSOURCING PROCESS

Introduction to Part I

If one single example were to be sought to illustrate the theme of this book, it could be taken from IBM Europe, whose director of procurement, John Gillett, told the authors that he intended 'to take out $1 billion in internal cost in one year'. In case there was any doubt about what he meant, he added, 'This means that last year's spend in the order of $10 billion becomes $9 billion this year'. He went on to say that this would achieve savings for IBM Europe of hundreds of millions of pounds each year.

Outsourcing played an important part in this huge re-engineering campaign which between 1989 and 1994 alone saw IBM's staffing levels reduced from 100 000 to 60 000. It also resulted in purchases doubling, contract staff reducing and the number of people serving IBM as outsource suppliers increasing from 1000 to 20 000.

A second example would be in the billions of pounds worth of internal work that the UK public service, through its Market Testing Programme, is attempting to hand over, complete with staff members, to private outsource providers.

What is going on here? Is this the re-engineered and re-invented world that is being talked about? Is it the rush to lean management, or a response to the ever increasing complexity of business processes? In an attempt to answer these questions, some of the trends which have been affecting how people live and work over the past 20 years will be discussed in Chapter 1.

Definition of outsourcing

A recent Mori survey of 50 top executives exhibited 'extensive ignorance' of outsourcing, despite the fact that more than 20 per cent of them were already actively considering the option.

Ferry de Kraker, Director General of the International Federation of Purchasing and Materials Management, gave the authors the following definition of outsourcing: 'Outsourcing really means finding *new suppliers* and *new ways* to secure the delivery of raw materials, goods, components and services. [It means that you] use the knowledge, experience and creativity of new suppliers which you did not use previously.' He felt that the term 'outsourcing' was itself too restrictive to describe what is really going on, and suggested such titles as 'lean management', 'sub-contracting', 'joint manufacture ventures', and 'co-makership'.

The outsource could be defined as a service outside the company acting as an extension of the company's business but responsible for its own management, while outsourcing could be defined as employing an outside agency to manage a function formerly carried on inside a company.

Paule Neale, Business Director of IBM's ISL company, describes outsourcing as the practice of handing over the planning, management and operation of certain functions to an independent third party.

The very spelling of the element of the outsource tends to vary. In other literature the outsource tends to be referred to as the outsourcer – that is someone who offers or operates an outsource service, which is not a good description, as we need also to refer to the company seeking an outsource as the outsourcer. We need to standardise our language. In this book, therefore, we refer to the outsource as the outsource supplier or provider.

To fully understand outsourcing, it must also be considered in the light of two other management decisions: the make it or buy it question and rightsizing, that is finding the right size, or the right number of staff, for an organisation (see Chapter 1). Both of these are central to the outsourcing decision.

Where new strategic alliances between suppliers and customers are replacing former adversarial roles between these two, outsourcing can achieve even more by eliminating difficult relationships between different departments within an organisation and allow the merging of departments. It is, however, a sensitive matter from the industrial relations point of view. Pierre Jocou, chief executive of the Car Quality Division of the proposed, but aborted, Renault–Volvo merged organisation, felt that the most important expertise used in the attempted merger was the human expertise (see Chapter 14).

The more specialised a business, the more likely it is that the expert help needed can be found only outside, rather than inside, the company. Trying to add an extra department, layers of management or information is not the best solution. The different departments within each organisation have less in common with each other than with similar departments in other companies, and indeed other countries. It is therefore easier to get expert help from outside. Even difficulties in sharing information between departments within a company can be eased by using an outside information technology resource.

Outsourcing is the increasingly common answer to the 'make it or buy it' question being asked by manufacturing industries and the 'do it ourselves or buy it in' question being asked by service industries.

The phenomenon of large corporations outsourcing even R & D to small companies has ended fears that large fortress-like cartels may gobble up all of industry and put small to medium sized enterprises (SMEs) out of business. These have a versatility and ingenuity which the larger companies need.

Outsourcing, combined with other techniques, is creating a whole new sophisticated environment for the customer–supplier activity. On the manufacturing front co-operation is intense with suppliers adopting the same systems as customers, sharing in those systems, becoming an extension of them, or taking over whole manufacturing systems from them. On the general management front whole business processes are being taken over.

This raises all the questions of agreements, relationships, qualification of suppliers, common practices, training and so on, but above all it calls for partnership.

Partnership

Purchasing managers worldwide, in the magazines of their national organisations, and through the publications of their international federation, have been using an expression not heard from them before. The term *'adversarial'* is being used in the context of their new non-adversarial relationships with their suppliers. The word is useful for a definition of partnerships as it expresses its opposite state.

The adversarial relationship was a reflection of the kind of selfish short-term practice which some people believed to be possible in a world of apparently endless resources, but which is no longer possible in a world where all parties in a trading relationship need to act in a responsible and caring manner.

'Partnership' is a much abused word in business today, and few organisations appear to understand what it really means. This helps to explain why so few companies have achieved successful partnership arrangements. These real partnerships, some arising from non-adversarial customer–supplier relations and many from new relationships, are the vehicles for the new successful outsourcing ventures.

Professor John C. Henderson of Boston University, who has carried out research into the nature of partnerships, defines partnership as follows: 'A strategy to achieve higher performance and/or lower costs through joint, mutually dependent action of independent organisations or individuals.' Partnerships are therefore about sharing risks and rewards, achieving common goals, and operating in mutual dependency.

The element of risk sharing makes partnerships strikingly different from the traditional customer–supplier relationship which excludes any possibility of risk, insisting, for example in cases of JIT (Just In Time) and shipping to point of use, on zero defects. Everything under an ISO 9000 standardised vendor system is guaranteed, and indeed often so under signed contract. Products are typically sold on the basis of specification (what it and its components are, how it will perform, to what limits and so on) and of price (how much it costs by amount purchased).

In the case of customer–supplier relationships, there may be little come back on the supplier, apart from warranty on product liability. A small supplier may therefore suddenly lose future business.

For example, should a supplier who has taken over information technology blame hardware or software for problems, he or she will get little sympathy from the customer.

Life was easier for in-house departments who bought all their technology from one large original equipment manufacturer (OEM) before deregulation and the proliferation of technology. For example, a single OEM might have supplied a company-wide telecommunications system or all computing hardware and soft-ware. These earlier OEMs had an interest in obtaining strategic commitments to their own technology, platforms or operating environments and used proprietary products and systems in an attempt to obtain and maintain monopolies. That world is now gone, chiefly through the emergence of standards.

The development of the trend in outsourcing in a number of areas, from a basic single service such as canteen management, buildings management or computing to more complex and wider ranging services such as telecommunications and administration, illustrates the evolution in the concept of partnerships with more and more responsibility being passed to the supplier. In the 1970s, for example, facilities management involved a supplier providing staff to an organisation to manage and operate a facility formerly operated by the company, such as a data processing department or a canteen. During the 1980s the practice of outsourcing saw that concept evolve to more of a partnership, while in the 1990s the trend is towards fuller partnerships where the outsource supplier becomes a real partner.

Outsourcing is a more customised service than facilities management and is based on achieving service levels set out in a service level agreement, while real partnerships are based on issues such as cultural fit – do they get on together, do they have a common purpose with shared rewards and shared risks?

Successful partnerships in outsourcing are therefore very different from the traditional customer–supplier relationship. A partnership can take up to a year to create and involve considerable management effort on both sides to ensure the relationship endures.

The following list shows the features of a partnership:

- senior management meet regularly
- payments relate to business outcome or specified level of performance rather than fixed work volumes
- a five-year or longer contract
- disclosure of costs and margins to each other
- each involved in the other's strategic planning
- difficulty in distinguishing between people in each company
- partner not selected on the basis of a competitive tendering process
- each partner looks for ways to reduce total costs
- each partner genuinely adds value.

One example of a successful partnership is that between the Body Shop and the Lane Group (see Chapter 16). Companies are increasingly setting up such partnership type arrangements in outsourcing supply. They require high levels of maturity. It is unusual, for example, for a company to open its books to its trucking company as the Body Shop does, but such openness is an essential element in accepting change. Because partners are by definition mutually interdependent, true partnerships will only come about where both parties understand what is involved and what the potential benefits are compared with the adversarial approach that still characterises many customer–supplier contracts.

Few partnerships are equal. The customer–supplier relationship has its own in-built conflict, but so have destructive power plays between managers of the same companies. The customer may want top quality but not want to pay for it, while the supplier may want to deliver the minimum and charge at the maximum rate. However the arrangement may be dressed up, it may be exploitive rather than a true partnership, and this can be true whether the partners are buying or selling ice-creams, cars or computer services. Simply calling it a 'partnership' will not, in itself, change the nature of the arrangement.

Some companies have tried to reflect these uncertainties by calling the arrangement 'co-sourcing'. This attempts to get round the changes that everyone knows will need to be managed during the life of a contract. Kodak's business, for example, changed to such an extent over a three-year period that it was necessary to renegotiate a five-year outsourcing contract with suppliers. A co-sourcing agreement can set out the parameters by which changes will be incorporated into a contract.

A further element in a partnership is mutuality of stake. Barclays Computer Operations (BCO), which is a wholly owned subsidiary of Barclays Bank, takes a mature view of the problem and has five key processes to manage a contract:

1 The account management team looking after the contract has 50 per cent of its bonus paid on customer satisfaction.
2 A technical refreshment clause ensures that 80 per cent of any cost benefits that arise from technical changes are passed directly back to the customer.
3 A total quality management system is operated jointly as a team effort.
4 They have a supplier users group which may be unique in the industry.
5 They operate pendulum arbitration which applies to any dispute, invoice, standard of service and so on. Normal arbitration encourages both sides to find the extreme position from which they will then be prepared to negotiate. This creates a difficult relationship between the two sides. Pendulum arbitration is a way of settling in favour of one side or the other – an all or nothing settlement. This encourages one party to work out what would be their minimum settlement and the

other to put their maximum offer on the table. BCO have never had cause to invoke this clause.

The future of outsourcing

Whether or not outsourcing is part of a larger movement, there is no doubt that the world of lean resources is dictating lean management; indeed human morality itself may have signalled the demise of waste, inefficiency and displays of opulence.

This book concentrates on the strategy of outsourcing from the point of view of the larger company which needs to look at that option, and attempts to provide a methodology for going about the difficult task of outsourcing. In a small number of cases the book looks at the strategies of outsource providers, as these also can be revealing. It was, however, difficult at times to separate the two as they are twin halves of a dynamic process which is changing the business world.

Several recent surveys quoted in the text reveal that outsourcing is growing while at the same time service providers are expanding their range of offerings. As this involves more concentration on core competencies by the principals who are passing this work to outside providers, this trend may also be a reflection of the fact that industry is coming to terms with a more demanding environment and a need to maximise resources and reduce waste.

1 The new drivers

There are a number of drivers behind the outsourcing process, many of them developments in world class techniques such as business process re-engineering, organisational restructuring, benchmarking, new alliances leading to more real partnerships and the whole process of leaner management, which is now also being both boosted and supported by standards and regulations.

Business process re-engineering

The concept of business process re-engineering is sweeping the business world and appears to apply equally to a large corporation, a one-person service, or an individual manager. It begins with an analysis of yourself, your strategy, your staff, the other people you work with, the technology you use, and the procedures or processes you employ to do the job.

The so-called 'drive for achieving excellence', sometimes called 'world class manufacturing', and which could as easily be called 'competing with the Japanese' or even 'staying in business', went hand in hand with the drive for quality and environmental

11

integrity. Costs and productivity were of paramount importance, focusing attention on the management function as never before. The total spend on activities, whether from outside or within, was examined carefully. Organisations were flattened to reduce hierarchical levels and buffers eliminated in the search for 'seamless processing'.

Michael Hammer deals with the subject in his book, *Re-engineering the Corporation* (1992, London: Nicholas Brealey). He believes every company should be looking for flexibility, the 'ability to adjust quickly to changing market conditions, lean enough to beat any competitor's price, innovative enough to keep its products and services technologically fresh, and dedicated enough to deliver maximum quality and customer service.' But too many companies believe that renewing their competitive abilities is simply a matter of getting their people to work harder, whereas the real issue is one of 'learning to work differently'. And this in turn means 'unlearning' much of what they know.

Most organisations today can trace their cultural origins back to the mode described by Adam Smith as the 'division of labour', which Henry Ford adopted and improved upon. Growing complexity in manufacturing demanded the more flexible approaches seen in the rise of so-called world class manufacturing with its emphasis on flexible manufacturing cells. A manager's or busy writer's version of one of these would be a round table with all the job files laid out around the circumference which rotates on demand, instead of a sequential production line – although instead of having a rotating table one could simply walk around it.

Another example of the need for flexibility in a business is when certain staff members cannot make progress on lower priority jobs. Those jobs stay always at the end of a queue and finally drop off altogether because they never get done. Middle managers make this worse as communications can get hopelessly confused, so what is needed are fewer managers and more flexible workers and systems.

According to Hammer, the demand for flexibility is also caused by the fact that 'nothing is constant or predictable – not market growth, customer demand, product life cycles, the rate of technological change, or the nature of competition.' Not even customer demand is staying the same, because now there are more choices, with products designed for specific or even unique needs. As he puts it, 'There is no longer any such notion as *the* customer. There is only *this* customer, the one with whom a seller is dealing at the moment and who now has the capacity to indulge his or her own personal tastes. The mass market has broken into pieces, some as small as a single customer.'

Even competition is no longer so simple. Hammer identifies competition of many different kinds, particularly because of niche markets. Competition can be on price, selection, quality or service.

Hammer defines re-engineering as 'the fundamental rethinking and radical redesign of business processes to achieve dramatic improvements in critical, contemporary measures of performance, such as cost, quality, service and speed.' He offers this further test: 'If I were re-creating this company today, given what I know and given current technology, what would it look like?'

Outsourcing as a re-engineering tool

It now begins to become clear why and where outsourcing will benefit from the re-engineering trend. Organisations which really are prepared to go back to square one and think about how best to produce, market and distribute a product or service will be forced to ask themselves what the best ways are of doing so, and at the same time whether they really need to own all the processes within their companies.

Re-engineering gives companies the opportunity to consider outsourcing as one of the tools that they can use in the new process – but re-engineering is easier described than done. The principles are sound but there are, as yet, few examples of dramatically successful re-engineering projects.

One of the reasons for this slow uptake is the internal resistance in organisations to such a potentially huge change (see Chapter 4). It means challenging powerful vested interests, who will find reasons for not making changes, at least for the moment or in their own areas. So outsourcing can actually be an easier route than internal re-engineering and can break this impasse. Indeed, out-source suppliers will often make their margins by re-engineering a process to make it more efficient after they have won the contract, as has happened in the UK's Market Testing Programme.

New companies or new business will take to outsourcing more readily than traditional organisations because they have the opportunity to properly engineer their business processes, to be the most efficient, and not just to copy others in the industry. Quotron, the new venture for Citibank, outsourced their world-wide network as they started in business.

New processes, which are designed for the task, have fewer stages where they can go wrong. The results are higher quality and fewer errors, and hence higher profits to the re-engineered operator.

David Andrews, head of the financial services division at Andersen Consulting which has forged pioneering co-operative sourcing deals with BP Exploration and the London Stock Exchange, says: 'Historically, senior management has concentrated on organising and managing a complex web of internal resources; but now a fundamental change is taking place. Driven by the need to focus on the customer, management has to think service, looking outwards to see how it can improve it. That's a completely different mindset. It requires you to ally in partnership with organisations expert in managing the people and the technology-intensive resources and business processes, which deliver service.'

How to analyse your business

So how do you carry out this analysis of yourself, your strategy, your staff, the other people you work with, the technology you use, and the procedures or processes you employ to do the job? Is what you are doing necessarily the correct or best thing in all cases? Is something getting too high a priority, while some other aspect of what you do, with a higher potential perhaps, is being neglected? Are you in the right business, or are there different services or products you should be in? Is your store selling the right products? Is there a service you can add to your existing services?

Once these first questions are asked, and perhaps partially answered, you then turn to the people with whom you are involved. There may be things some people are doing that are better done by others. Have you defined people's jobs too rigidly – the secretary's, the driver's, one employee doing the A work, the next the B? Is the job description causing demarcation and rigidity? Perhaps a change in job description, or its total elimination, could produce a miracle of diversification.

You should then move on to the process. Are you doing it right? If someone is fussing and upset at work, suggest that he or she takes a look at re-engineering the procedures. Something is not right. Fuss is concerned with non-work areas; it is not related to real work. It is connected to the lost document, the bad schedule, absenteeism of staff. The elimination of fuss and hassle makes more time for real valuable work.

Value re-engineering

The Andersen Consulting people are finding that re-engineering is a booming business for them, and their 20 per cent growth rate per annum over the past four years illustrates this. Andrew Hunter, a partner in Andersen Consulting in Europe, explained that the process is actually 'value driven re-engineering' and these values can come from product, process, customer, environment or staff.

Value engineering of products has been around for years – witness, the marvellously re-engineered portable computers – but now we find whole businesses being value re-engineered.

The Andersen formula

We asked Andrew Hunter how it is done. The Andersen formula is: first, interview the customer, second, ask the employees and then consider such aspects as the social agenda and legislation. In other words, first the *vision*, then the *alignment*, that is whether what we do at the moment is out of line with the vision. Such issues as how new staff are recruited as well as where time or resources are being wasted will be involved at this stage.

Next comes the *master plan*, or what you intend to do about it, and finally a programme of *implementation* in what Andrew Hunter calls 'digestible chunks'. At recent seminars, Andersen have found that the process received responses from a wide spectrum – at one extreme, from a multinational deciding to close depots, and at the other, from a one-man professional who finally came to see the disadvantageous impact of a random workload on his business, and started to operate on a planned basis.

When questioned about whether technology was the driving force behind the new approach, Andrew Hunter replied, 'Clearly, technology is involved, especially in the time compression part, but the process itself is fundamental also in the time it takes and the potential for mistakes – chiefly through what are being called the "buffers".' The buffers are the unnecessary human or other physical interfaces within a process, perhaps even a wire basket for accumulating enquiries.

Asked why they were not a problem before, since there is nothing new about buffers, he replied, 'Because we didn't think buffers were bad.' He explained that they are bad because 'a buffer is caused by potential for error'. So this means hedging your bets, producing two versions in case one fails, inspecting after the error, instead of getting it right first time.

The process of continuous improvement is one of finding the mistakes and eliminating the buffers to which the mistakes are related. As Hunter puts it, 'Buffers don't cause mistakes; they are there because of mistakes. Take the mistake out and then you can take the buffer out.' How many of you have searched for that bank statement or notice of withholding tax because you could not remember where you filed it? Think of how much fuss and curses you could save by having it filed properly in the first instance.

While the process began in manufacturing, it now has huge implications for the service sector. This is reflected in the Andersen client list, which includes both the government and private sector. Banks, insurance companies, welfare departments and hospitals must simplify processes, almost clarify them. It is fundamental for customer service, and it is going to decide who stays in business.

A recent edition of an Andersen newsletter discusses the four elements of strategy, people, processes and technology, and puts them in the context of a change programme that must be managed to a timetable. This is to make sure that the changes are also consistent with what is being demanded by the constituency of customer, shareholder, community, staff or other relevant demander of change.

Time compression
In certain businesses the new world of time compression is demanding high technology – computers, word processors, spell checking software, hard disks, electronic transmission and so on – if the reduced lead times are to be met. Companies that have them and can use them will be in business, given that they get everything else right; companies that do not have them will not survive. Those that stay in business, however, will get much more of the action as suppliers are reducing in number, fewer and fewer obtaining more and more work. This is as true for journalists with modems as it is for component suppliers using electronic data interchange (EDI).

Andersen itself tries to cope with the needs to re-engineer its processes, and they claim to do this both locally and globally. At least once a year the local team should stand back and look both at what it is doing and what its clients are doing, while on a global basis the company has a strategy of periodic fundamental review.

Value chain analysis
Another approach, or perhaps another name for the evaluation process, is value chain analysis. This is based on the concept of a *value chain*, and it is described in Michael E. Porter's book *Competitive Advantage* (1994, New York: The Free Press).

This is how he describes a value chain: 'The value chain desegregates a firm into its strategically relevant activities in order to understand the behaviour of costs and the existing and potential sources of differentiation. A firm gains competitive advantage by performing these strategically important activities more cheaply or better than its competitors.'

The value chain also allows you to identify *components* of the business that may be eligible candidates for outsourcing. The value chain shows the linkage of these components to other parts of the organisation, the role they play and the basis for deciding whether they are strategic, a source of competitive advantage or an operation that needs to be performed at maximum efficiency or lowest cost.

A value chain can

- provide a common understanding of a logical business structure
- determine the source of competitive advantage – cost, differentiation, competitive scope
- identify opportunities for organisational change
- identify business opportunities
- serve as a communications tool as well as a management framework.

Organisational restructuring

Throughout the corporate world, and now in some countries at government level, layers of management are being reduced ('flattening of the organisation') and the distance between the chief executive and the shop floor worker is being shortened. This vertical process is matched by the horizontal processes of the elimination of buffers and the blurring of boundaries between customer and suppliers, with outsourcing moving them from the traditional customer–supplier roles to that of strategic business partnership.

The expression 're-inventing' has appeared, for example, in the UK in the context of re-inventing government through the Market Testing Programme. This re-invention is part of the global process discussed on page 10 of trying to come up with a leaner and more responsive and productive organisation.

Competition

If IBM intends to shed £1 billion in internal overheads, then Digital Equipment Co. Ltd and others must follow. Lean and efficient companies become the benchmarks for others to follow.

Never before was it truer that in order to survive, companies must keep up with the competition.

Changing technology

When the European automotive manufacturing industry was faced with incorporating a brand new technology, such as electronics for new automobile controls, into its products, it had the clear choice of learning to do this itself or outsourcing it to an existing expert contract manufacturer already doing similar work for the computer industry (see page 151).

Computer users are also faced with an accelerating rate of change in information technology as well as whole new application areas such as super highways and multimedia, both of which will soon be commonplace.

Costs

In 1993 the UK's Inland Revenue signed a ten-year outsourcing contract worth more than one thousand million pounds with EDS, in the expectation that it would reduce its information technology costs by well over 50 per cent. This was the largest ever outsourcing deal in the UK.

At the same time, the second largest took place as British Aerospace signed a ten-year contract worth almost £900 million with Computer Sciences Corporation (CSC), also in the expectation of substantial cost savings.

The Inland Revenue deal was the most dramatic result to date of the government's Market Testing Programme (see Chapter 8). The press release announcing the billion pound outsourcing contract had this to say: 'The Inland Revenue now believes it can make significant further improvement in the quality and value for money of its work through a strategic contract with EDS.'

Two partners were happy. Less happy were other consortia bidding for the contract, who, collectively, had spent millions on their bids and ended up as also-rans.

The new alliances

Today's customer–supplier relationships are changing from what were adversarial roles to those of beneficial partnerships. The Japanese car manufacturers made rapid strides against their European competitors by forming strategic alliances with single component suppliers, while the Europeans carried on their tradition of multisourcing parts for lowest cost and security of supply.

The single biggest change in the supplier–customer interface is the tendency to buy all parts and services in one category from one supplier and to form a partnership so close with the supplier that both share the same system. It is as if an employee sets up in premises outside the plant and is paid on invoice rather than by payroll.

This close alliance creates other demands on the supplier, such as the need to participate in similar systems of production and communication and even management. An extreme example of this is where the customer is operating in the mode known as *kanban*, which is sell one-make one, and the supplier and customer are required to respond to market demands simultaneously.

The most sophisticated manifestation of this system is when the supplier shares the same electronic marketing network as the customer, so that a re-order sent from a European warehouse is read in both customer and supplier plants at the same time.

Shared systems mean shared standards, and ISO 9000 is now the norm for the quality management systems required. It is already expected of most suppliers and it will soon be a minimum requirement. In the years ahead companies will increasingly achieve the new environment standard, and the demand for this also will be passed down to suppliers. Buyers have become interested not just in their suppliers' quality and environmental standards, but also in their health and safety procedures. Sub-contractors operating on customers' premises will have to produce evidence that their own staff have been trained in the new regulations.

Some suppliers have what are known as focused plants – that is they dedicate whole production lines and even factories to one customer. The overall expression for this from the customer's point of view is 'central management – focused supply'.

Many companies do not outsource their 'core competencies', or the core business which makes their products; some, however, outsource even these. IBM at first glance appears to be willing to outsource everything, from its hardware to its own management, but there are some aspects of its business that it will not part with (see Chapter 17).

The new world, where efficiency and productivity were trying to accommodate quality in the 'fitness for purpose' sense and environmental integrity, could no longer tolerate cutthroat business relationships. The adversarial relationships had to give way to co-operation and true partnerships.

National policy

In his book *Reinventing the Factory II* (1992, New York: The Free Press) Roy Harmon predicts a revolution in transport and warehousing, with the former carrying bulk commodities only and the latter virtually eliminated. This, the author claims, will be achieved by the cluster principle, whereby factories house suppliers close to their customers.

He predicts that these clusters will also service the local or regional market, so that long transport runs and warehousing of finished products will be eliminated. Many national industrial development agencies are now trying to develop infrastructures in which the so-called 'linkage' principle will apply – that is large companies buying components and services locally from within the cluster.

In some smaller economies it is simply not possible to develop an industrial base which is all embracing. Indeed, even international companies are finding that they have to look overseas for strategic partnerships and alliances.

Industrial development agencies, particularly those in the smaller countries developing local small- to medium-sized enterprises, see outsourcing from large foreign-owned and indigenous manufacturers as potentially powerful local industrial catalysts.

To this end they have been trying to ensure that their territories contain all the support elements necessary in the new cluster environment.

The development agencies believe that the stimulation of linkages can have a profound, beneficial effect on the industrial fabric of an economy in many ways from direct purchasing of local products and services to paying wages and spin off in technology and ideas. Should the principals, who are mostly multinationals, also increase local outsourcing, the local benefits will increase.

Public procurement within the European Union

One of the biggest drivers in the new outsourcing trend should have been the opening up of public procurement within the European Union. In reality it has had mixed effects.

Public procurement within the EU is the purchasing by state authorities, central governments, local agencies and state enterprises. Before the legislation which opened up procurement for all of these, a very small percentage, as low as 2 per cent according to some commentators, was bought outside national boundaries. The thresholds above which the contracts must be offered to any bidder in the EU are as low as ECU 200 000 for supplies and services, and ECU 5 000 000 for public works such as construction projects. The European Commission has vigorously pursued the objective of opening up this market and the last bastion, services, fell to outside competition in the middle of 1993.

The European Commission has also made the rules of competing for public business as clear as possible, eliminated red tape and encouraged those who feel excluded to complain if the public buyers appear to be breaking the rules. With the value of public procurement over £455 billion, or 15 per cent of total Union GDP (gross domestic product), this is very big business indeed. For example, the UK spent 21 per cent of GDP on public procurement, most of it at home, before the opening up of this market.

The main elements of public procurement from the point of view of prospective suppliers are public works, such as buildings and roads; public supplies in the form of goods, which is virtually everything bought by public buyers; some of the formerly excluded sectors of telecommunications, energy, drinking water supply and transport; and, last but not least, services.

So why the qualification in the first lines of this section about public procurement being a huge driver for outsourcing? There are at least two reasons. The first is that these new measures have simply forced public buyers to accept tenders from suppliers in other member states. The second, which is more significant, is that the red tape, chiefly the highly formalised tender and contractual procedures central to a public procurement activity, mitigates against the kind of open and informal alliance fundamental to the kinds of real partnerships which are emerging in private sector outsourcing.

Over and above the EU drive to open up public procurement, the UK government has embarked upon its programme of Market Testing (see Chapter 8). This is outsourcing in its truest sense and displays many of the characteristics which public procurement within the European Union lacks.

The changing world of work

The changing rules which govern supplier management are also changing the world of work itself. This in turn is being affected by another related trend – that of self employment in the freelance or contract sense.

These changing rules are causing dramatic changes in the world of work. The terms 'unemployment' and 'full employment', the latter in the sense of a permanent pensionable job, are no longer applicable in a world where part-time, freelance and contract work are on the increase and are blurring the boundaries of full employment and unemployment. This affects information processing (see Chapter 9), administration and the whole business process (see Chapter 10), buildings management (see Chapter 11), catering (see Chapter 13), and contract manufacturing (see Chapter 12) amongst others. In a number of cases, such as contract manufacturing, recent growth in the market for outsourcing exceeds that of growth in the industry itself.

The practice of facilities management, or outsourcing, is now one of the biggest growth areas, if not the biggest. It extends over information technology – its biggest sector – estates, the selling of serviced space, buildings and related services and service provision, although it is hard to categorise these rigidly.

An interesting trend is the way the successful outsource providers are constantly expanding the range of their services, for example, providers of routine information technology processing services are expanding their offerings to take over the whole business process. Gardner Merchant, who began with canteens and moved on to a huge range of offerings, is an outstanding example (see Chapter 13).

Summary

Rather than being a haphazard process, the development of outsourcing is the inevitable result of the many new and increased pressures on industry and on all of the resources of a world where internal buffers and layers of management can no longer be afforded. The process is being driven both by demand, as management seeks better ways of doing routine work, and by the providers of the outsourced services, who offer to take on more and more of their customers' workloads.

2   Make it or buy it?

The make it or buy it decision is fundamental to the process of outsourcing. 'Making it' also assumes 'doing it' or 'servicing it', as it applies to the provision of services too. The question can apply both to companies and to individuals. How many of you, for example, would be better handing over some of the things you do to others, leaving you more time for the vital aspects of the job?

The make it or buy it question

Central to both outsourcing decisions and to the management of supply is the make it or buy it question. This is proving to be another example of how thinking about multinationals and monopolies is changing. There used to be a belief that the great cartels would exclude smaller enterprises and individuals from the market, that big was strong, that economies of scale out-weighed enterprise, and that such creative processes as research and development belonged only to the mighty.

It is clear now to those who have worked for large corporations or government departments that enterprise can flourish if people escape from what appeared to be a bastion of security into the heady environment of positive action and success.

Out in the open marketplace, former constraints are more sharply defined and recognised for what they were. A large, highly formalised internal organisation can, and often does, stifle, stultify and strangle good new ideas, and even necessary positive work, if for no other reason than the existence of the job description, or the job definition.

The entrepreneurs

Mature entrepreneurs have found that proposed activities, which had been turned down by an employer in the last years of their employment, became the basis of their new enterprises in the open market bringing considerable financial reward. The proposals for such activities were not so much turned down by former managers, as by colleagues who ensured that job definitions were honoured. They were probably not even aware of the corporate loss which resulted. They may have genuinely believed, for example, that the public relations manager should not engage in developing new services, that the laboratory technician should not sell company publications, and that the librarian should not develop new markets for the technology transfer process. The job descriptions both enshrined rights and defended against encroachment.

Looking in retrospect from self employment back to the world of employment, the separate roles within organisations can seem even more adversarial than those in a traditional or bad customer–supplier relationship. This gives rise to interesting thoughts about the nature of competition.

Destructive competition

Competition is a bit like advice and criticism – it can be constructive and destructive. Even within organisations a certain amount of competitive activity is necessary, but it must not be destructive or negative to the objectives of the organisation. What becomes quickly apparent is that destructive competition increases with the size of the organisation. However, it can be reduced virtually to zero in small companies where all share the same goals with enthusiasm.

Destructive competition is practically non-existent in a healthy customer–supplier relationship, making this potentially the most positive and profitable of all relationships and one in which the goals are truly common and where each makes common cause with the other.

The make it or buy it decision begins with the organisation itself. The point where destructive competition may begin has to be defined. There are, of course, many devices which can be employed inside organisations to reduce the rot of destructive competition such as certain manufacturing and management techniques, but with increasing size it is only a matter of time before this weakness of humanity will exhibit itself or be manifested through decreasing profitability.

The regulated market

An increasingly regulated market is also affecting this decision, particularly with such burdens as increasing social legislation – an example is the UK reaction to the social chapter of the Maastricht Treaty. As the better-off countries of Europe pressed for increased worker rights, putting greater burdens on employers, they seemed unaware of the irony that the very pressure to better so-called 'permanent and pensionable' employment was in fact encouraging employers to employ fewer and outsource more. It also had the bizarre effect of reducing the pool of workers prepared to accept low pay, so there were workers on the dole in the poorer countries who were not interested in marginal jobs. In the US a huge labour force is available at the unskilled end of the market, from fast-food workers to window cleaners, but in a country of high unemployment in Europe it was difficult to find anyone to mow a lawn or paint a shed.

In this European environment the much criticised 'black economy' has also expanded. An unemployed person on the dole may not be interested in the prospect of earning money in a low paid job. However, entrepreneurs have appeared with vans and ladders and are available for any job from fixing roofs to washing windows – all on a cash basis of course, and they operate out of the back of the van rather than from a taxable office.

Deciding on the optimum size

The first decision in the make it or buy it dialogue may be to select the optimum size of each corporate enterprise. This can be facilitated by breaking down large organisations into business centres, separate companies, or even focused sub-plants, so that former supervisors become managers and each employee receives more of what is now being called 'empowerment'.

Many thinkers and commentators are encouraging more empowerment for workers, while others warn that too much empowerment will create anarchy. Perhaps the management science of the 21st century will concern itself with defining the optimum sized commercial enterprise as well as quantifying, or at least devising tools for identifying and measuring, destructive work practices. The prohibition of such practices can then join quality and environmental integrity in the list of necessary attributes of facilitative industry.

One result of this kind of decision making is that many managers will be forced to face the question of whether they themselves should leave employment and take certain functions outside as self-employed sub-contractors. Studies of enterprise have identified employment as the single largest source of business ideas for emerging entrepreneurs, for example, components and services which the employer is currently producing in-house could be provided from outside; components and services being bought from outside could be provided to the company and other companies by an internal manager who has become self-employed; components and services which the company is not involved in, but could or should be, could again be provided from outside.

The process of ascertaining the optimum number to be employed may be called identifying the 'magic number'. All self-employed people know that, except where they have key specialised skills, the number is greater than one. In most work situations, more than one person in the team means the team now has the ability both to specialise and to achieve some economies of scale.

The most powerful division of labour may be that between production and selling. Another powerful partnership is that between innovator and administrator, particularly where the good innovator is a partner to, or supported by, a good administrator. An almost perfect commercial balance is achieved by good innovation, supported by production, good selling and careful administration.

Most companies trying to identify the optimum number of staff will already be working enterprises with products, services and markets. For these companies outsourcing will be one way of establishing both the core competencies and the magic number to be employed in the company, although it will be easier for a new company to do this than for an existing one with established staff and practices.

Advantages of the buy it decision

Outsourcing is recognised as a vital mechanism for stimulating local employment through what are known as national linkages; however, one has yet to see any government admit that outsourcing is also a method of reducing employment. While some countries are busy welcoming outside buyers who come to purchase components, the host countries of those buyers may not welcome the running down of their local staffs.

The new customer–supplier relationship is healthy because each shares the same objectives. The freedom the small supplier has to get things done without organisational red tape also creates more freedom for the customer who can now get on with more important tasks. With specific and repetitive functions gone outside, core demands can be more fully addressed.

Above all, however, the employment of outsiders and the fresh, new dialogue which can ensue give rise to creativity and to a potentiality or spontaneity hitherto difficult to achieve. The maintenance of the *status quo* within large organisations, on the other hand, will eventually breed lethargy and boredom, a corporate mediocrity and finally the demise of the enterprise – nowadays, given reduced cycle times, sooner rather than later.

For decades people believed that only mighty corporations could do certain things, such as making automobiles, aircraft and consumer goods. This is still true in the sense that small operators on their own cannot make such things, as they lack the economies of scale. However, outsourcing means that small operators can participate in products subject to economies of scale.

What has happened is that the advantages of economies of scale have been balanced by what might be called 'paralysis of movement' as bureaucratic management structures have made creativity and flexibility difficult to achieve. New processes, such as the flattening of organisations, the removal of buffers and closer links with suppliers, have helped to ensure that the buy it decision can be more favourable than the make it, except where gigantic economies of scale are involved, as with automated factories, steel mills and shipyards.

Another positive result of the decision to buy outside can be the creativity and sharing achieved at the design stage of a new product. IBM, for example, finds that, as it can now telescope a process by working in parallel with a number of outsiders, design times are greatly reduced.

Outsourcing to small contractors reduces the ability of unions to hold up production, and decreases the power generally of internal troublemakers. Forty years of bus strikes and holding a population to ransom have resulted from the Irish government's reluctance to outsource public transport to private operators.

In-house politics are not confined to unions; managers intent on private gain at company expense also practise destructive power politics. The customer–supplier relationship is far healthier as each shares the other's objectives.

Frustration is the spring-board of enterprise and many a supplier gets a start by leaving an employer and doing something for that employer from outside better than it could have been done inside.

The ability of any enterprise to cope effectively beyond a certain size is a fundamental issue in productivity which must be addressed. As one manager put it, 'You can only fit so many usable brains under one roof'.

Analysing the make it or buy it issue

Here is a structured way of evaluating the 'make it or buy it' question:

1 Evaluate your time
How much valuable management time is being spent on non-core activities? To answer this, list the core activities then the non-core, and estimate how much time is spent on each in a typical week/year.

2 Skills supplement
What useful skills could you buy in that could enhance your business? Identify skilled people in potential suppliers whose talents and entrepreneurial drive has brought them there.

3 Identify your utilities
What internal business is just a utility capable of being out-sourced?

4 Cash and capital ratios
Identify the potential for cash and capital flows and their new uses.

5 Space and people
What is your right size in terms of people? What are your space considerations? (Would alternative available space allow a reduction in number of buildings or sites?)

6 Products/services
Can these be expanded? Should they be reduced?

7 How well are you really operating?
Carry out the benchmarking exercises in Chapter 3.

Summary

The advantages of economies of scale have been negated by 'paralysis of movement' in many bureaucratic companies. They are now assessing the effects of overstaffing and inflexibility, and discovering downsizing and the magic number of people.

Increasing social legislation will add to the motivation to outsource as employers try to reduce such burdens. The outside supplier will be an attractive alternative to permanent and pensionable staff.

Outsourcing is a mechanism for acquiring new dialogue, ideas, creativity and potentiality. The supplier may have more freedom to get things done, to do them better and cheaper, and to give more customer satisfaction.

In-house politics and frustration are reduced and the customer–supplier relationship is healthy as the partners have common cause. Management can give more attention to the core competencies.

3 Benchmarking

The concept of the benchmark is as old as industry itself. Somebody else, either in the same or a similar industry, may be doing things a better way. There may be more than one benchmark. The benchmark for the purposes of assessing outsourcing prospects is one or more companies which operate at desirable levels of quality, efficiency, and profitability. All the better if they have also outsourced successfully, although the benchmark may be used in the first instance to re-engineer a company's processes.

Care must be taken when finding out about competitors as there may be legal constraints. If it is not possible to get permission to talk with a potential benchmark, there are a number of international services offering information on companies.

Looking not so much at the whole company, but at its products and processes may be the most practical way to benchmark.

The benchmarking process

The most talked about benchmark user is Xerox Corporation, which was in big trouble in the late 1970s as Japanese importers undermined its US home market for photocopiers. Xerox was experiencing that 'economy of scale' which produces paralysis and inefficiency. In the early 1980s the company embarked upon its benchmarking project, selecting key service processes, such as those which could contribute to bottlenecks in manufacturing or delivery, specifically packing and shipping.

The story goes that Xerox saw an article in the US magazine *Modern Materials Management* about a new computerised picking system at the L.L. Bean company in Freeport Maine, and followed this up with a benchmarking request. This exercise was so successful that it revolutionised the way Xerox set about its order filling, and the company began a programme of hundreds of benchmarking studies under full-time benchmarking managers.

By the end of the 1980s the Xerox chief executive officer, David Kearns, was reporting labour costs down by 50 per cent, materials down 40 per cent, and customer satisfaction up almost 40 per cent. In addition, the company captured the top US national quality prize, known as the Malcolm Baldridge Award, in 1989, ten years after almost going out of business (see David Kearns, 1992, *Prophets in the Dark*, Harper-Business).

After identifying the benchmark, the purpose is to find out what, if any, outsourcing they have done, are doing or plan to do. If they have outsourced certain functions and performance has improved, you will need to examine your own prospects in this regard. A good example here would be an airline which as a result of outsourcing flight information has improved both financial performance and customer service.

As Pierre Jocou of Renault points out (see Chapter 14), there can be more than one benchmark. Renault used several different competitive automobile manufacturers to benchmark for different functions. You could take customer service from one, design from a second, market growth from a third, and so on. You should also look for other activities which might explain success (see comments on London Insurance on page 160). A superior company may have outsourced, but some other factor could have caused its recent success. It may be possible to build an 'ideal' benchmark with pieces from different companies, but such a benchmark should be treated as having a short shelf life.

The big question is how to obtain the kinds of confidential information needed to form a benchmark from most companies, particularly from competitors? Hiring key people from the competition is a good start, but the legal warnings on page 40 should be heeded. There are other useful indicators which will be considered next.

International companies

ISO 9000

An increasingly useful indication is whether or not the company is registered to ISO 9000. The ISO (International Standards Organisation) does not operate a registration scheme, so registration will be from an approved registration body, this may be a national standards agency or an established private body, such as Britain's BSI (British Standards Institute) or SGS (Société Générale de Surveillance), the large private, Swiss headquartered, certification and testing agency.

It is important to appreciate that a company can operate to the ISO 9000 standard, which is a standard for quality management systems, and not be registered as doing so by an independent third party, as certification may not be demanded by customers. The process of registration, while spreading rapidly worldwide, has only just commenced in a number of countries.

In the UK, Ireland and Australia registration to the ISO 9000 standard is quite advanced. The following categories of companies should be registered:

- all large manufacturers in the engineering, food and drinks, electronics and general manufacturing sectors
- most sub-suppliers of components and sub-systems to the above companies

Several categories of companies may operate to even higher levels of performance where other standards are demanded. These may be certified to those other standards rather than to ISO 9000 while still having achieved ISO 9000. These include:

- pharmaceutical manufacturers registered by government departments of health
- chemical companies operating to chemical industry standards
- automotive component manufacturers, operating to standards set by manufacturers such as Ford or Toyota
- suppliers to the nuclear industry
- manufacturers of aerospace components and systems.

In the case of all of the above, the test is simple. If they are supplying components and products, they have to be state of the art, certified companies in order to be able to do business in the developed world.

In the US, Canada, Pacific Rim, the balance of Europe outside the UK and Ireland and a number of countries, such as Malaysia, the ISO 9000 test was introduced later but is growing rapidly – for example, at 150 per cent per annum in the US and Japan and at 100 per cent in Germany.

Most countries have national registers of certified companies and virtually all registered companies display their logo, not on their product but on headed paper and other media.

Environmental management standard

A second quality excellence benchmark indicator is emerging, and this is the new environmental management standard, the number of which is BS 7750 in the UK, AFNOR X 30–200 in France and IS 310 in Ireland. There will be an ISO version of these sometime in the near future. It is virtually certain that all companies adopting the environmental management standard will already be certified to ISO 9000, so they will be performing to what is being referred to as an 'ultimate standard' of quality, environmental integrity, staff health and safety, public safety and product safety. Such companies will make excellent benchmarks as it is difficult to imagine them adopting such good codes of practice at the expense of profitability. All the practices under the standards involve precise specifications, full delivery to customer requirements, environmental integrity and safety of product and process. The combined standards also reduce waste and costly re-runs.

Other factors to research

In addition to quality and environmental probity, you will also need access to information on financial performance. Agencies such as Moody's Investors Service supply in-depth analysis of the financial performance of individual companies, while public companies and those on the Fortune 500 and 1000 lists also publicise performance.

Moodys has around 10 000 public companies on file, as well as many other categories including banks, and can give analyses on competitive components and keep track of market trends and profitability. It offers to locate new business prospects and to research competitors. It even offers a service to establish conflicts of interest with attorneys. Moodys began in this business in 1901 when John Moody published his *Manual of Industrial and Corporation Securities*, which was probably the world's first directory of public companies. Its offspring are still available in bound manuals, but are also updated weekly and accessible in microfiche and on CD-ROM.

Moodys *International Manual* service offers to locate new suppliers, track the financial performance of competitors or potential partners, help to make informed purchasing or credit decisions, or analyse new market opportunities. In those territories where Moodys does not operate directly, it can be contacted through such partner companies as Dun & Bradstreet.

Public relations ratings are also important. What do its customers or ex-customers think of a company? A little research done here through direct calls to both customers and ex-customers could be important.

You should also find out whether or not the proposed benchmark company has a good or a bad record of employee relations. This is particularly significant if strikes or employee dissent accompanied an outsourcing or downsizing decision. Wyatt, the US research company, reported many bad downsizing decisions which had paid no dividends because employees were badly treated.

European companies

Within the European Union the ISO 9000 award and the environmental management standards (see page 35) can be used to identify good companies. These will shortly allow European companies to demonstrate compliance with a prestigious EU Eco management and audit scheme regulation, which requires the implementation of an environmental management system to a standard such as those listed.

Another very important distinction for certain categories of companies selling in Europe is whether they have a CE Mark. The CE Mark on a product is now compulsory for all companies selling toys, machinery, construction components, telecom equipment, medical appliances and personal protective equipment. The CE Mark denotes that the product conforms to essential requirements, such as all regulations and standards, and it is a passport to European markets.

US companies

In the US the importance of the Malcolm Baldridge Award for quality may be replaced by achievement of the international ISO 9000 standard; indeed, ISO supporters outside North America are less impressed by such provincialism as they are by an international quality mark.

US companies whose systems and products are certified to quality or other standards can be asked if the certifications are from reputable certification agencies? You can also ask if the company has a good or bad environmental track record – has it, for example, been fined under the Superfund levy, which is the US legislation making companies responsible for all environmental incidents, past as well as present?

The process/product as the key to benchmarking

Perhaps the most practical way to benchmark against either potential partner companies or competitors is to do it by process or product.

Starting with the product, supposing you wanted to benchmark your electric motor against those of the competition, how do you begin? Simply by going out, all over the world if necessary, and buying the products of your competitors. Back at the work bench you take them to pieces to determine the number of components and the probable cost of the materials and labour. You also test run each for efficiency and output. Once you have set the range of part numbers, costs and outputs, you set your own against these and decide the point to which you want to relate. The results could mean fewer components and less cost for your model or better performance for customers.

The process examined can be anything from the practice of outsourcing itself to the operation of the administration or the maintenance function, but be sure that, as in the case of the product, you choose comparable companies. These could include:

- all competitors
- companies in the same sector with a non-competing but comparative product range, for example, in the engineering sector an electric motor manufacturer could look at a pump manufacturer of the same size, while in the electronics industry a power supply manufacturer could look at a telecom component manufacturer
- companies in different sectors but with the same process – any company can look at any other company's canteen or buildings management facility
- in the case of service companies, the key processes such as level of service and distribution mechanisms are easy to identify, for example delivery times.

Methodology for the benchmarking process

1 Decide on the benchmark:
   - a suitable company already outsourcing
   - a product
   - a process

- all the above.
2 Assign responsibility to a project leader or consultant. This can be the first step or in parallel with the above. This will also be a part of the overall methodology proposed for the outsourcing project discussed in Appendix IV.
3 Carry out the analysis of the process suggested in Appendix IV.
4 Design a template or questionnaire to select questions and answers about the benchmark company's process.
5 If you are choosing a company which is not a competitor and hoping to get its co-operation, avoid those well-known names which will be fed up with similar requests. Use services such as Moodys to help at this stage. A good technical or business freelance journalist or a specialised consultant knows how to use telephone and database access to make this part of the job easier.
6 Visit the benchmark if you have permission or begin the comparisons.
7 Analyse the data, in particular looking for differences in performance, seeking both inhibiting and facilitating practices.
8 Use the knowledge of the inhibiting and facilitating practices to amend your own process or make recommendations to management.

The legalities involved

Ironically, you are in greater danger of breaking the law if you benchmark openly with a willing partner than if you carry out industrial espionage. Here, for example, are some questions which companies benchmarking with each other in the US need to consider:

- Could you find yourself in discussions which could be interpreted as price fixing, restraint of trade, insider trading or unlawful acquisition of trade secrets?
- Have you signed confidentiality or non-disclosure agreements?

- Can the information gained be passed on to any other person or company, for example to a competitor of the benchmark company by one of your team going to work for them?

Summary

Select your company or companies with some of your processes in mind. More processes worth looking at may emerge when you begin to study your benchmark. Once you have permission or know the legalities of what you propose to do, go through the methodology outlined above. Above all, keep an open mind and do not let people tell you that the benchmark can do things that no one else can do. This may be your opportunity to make a great breakthrough. The benchmark can also reveal whether you are going to survive the way you are; it could act as an early warning system.

4 Possible pitfalls

Introduction

It is easy to assume that outsourcing is a well trodden path, but many outsourcing relationships go wrong, and this chapter discusses some of the reasons. There is no one single aspect of an outsourcing relationship that can be blamed: it is a complex business management relationship, usually uniquely constructed to satisfy a set of circumstances and often the first time that an organisation has entered into such an agreement.

Treating outsourcing as a high level project

Appendix IV suggests a project methodology for the process of outsourcing. Some examples which show that it can be the most important project ever taken on by any company are the Xerox story (see page 33), the enormous changes at IBM (see Chapter 17), the UK government's Market Testing Programme (see Chapter 8), and the many other case studies. It could make projects, such as that gone through to adopt the ISO 9000 standard, seem small by comparison. It could revolutionise the way a company is structured and operates.

The project needs high status, a project leader, top management authorisation, and, if there are internal management difficulties as there are almost certain to be, an outside consultant.

Establishing the real costs

Whatever the relationship on offer, whether customer–supplier, partnership or joint venture, the provider of the outsourced service has done it before, whereas the company embarking on the venture for the first time has not. 'Trust but verify' is what Ronald Reagan is supposed to have said with regard to the Russian arms reduction treaties.

Potential traps include a price-escalation clause, through which suppliers can make high profits from the index-linking of contracts. Inflation at 15 per cent a year and technology prices falling at 20 per cent gave huge scope for profits in the late 1980s. The actual costs must be identified, both of providing the service in house at today's prices and buying it from an outsource today and in three years' time. This is fundamental if a primary motivation is to reduce operational costs.

Many companies do not know how much the function under scrutiny is actually costing them. This may be because it is widely decentralised, as in the cases of administration, energy and information processing. For example, companies could get close to establishing real costs when all accounting and IT were centralised, but even then there were varying views on how much corporate overhead had to be included. Now distributed systems, departmental and divisional autonomy, empowerment of lower levels in the organisation and the spread of the PC and networks make the task virtually impossible.

You also need to watch out for the loose financial arguments. 'Our proposal will mean that you save the cost of your maintenance department' may assume that you could do something useful with a building which is custom-designed to facilitate maintenance activities only.

Outsource providers make money from changes, and the one certainty in most organisations today is that nothing is certain. A survey in the *Harvard Business Review* some years ago looked at the five-year plans drawn up by the Fortune 500 companies. Out of the 500, 486 made *radical* changes to their plans. So how can this be built into a five-year outsourcing contract?

Specific pitfalls

Some specific pitfalls follow which have been grouped under business, people and technology.

Business
Business is in a constant state of change. The following possibilities need to be considered:

New line of business
What happens if and when you develop a new line of business? How will this be incorporated into the contract with the outsource supplier? Should it be kept separate? Do you engage in a new tendering process which includes the present supplier?

Business downturn
Have you considered the possibility that the business volumes on which you have based the outsourcing contract will decline? Have you assessed the range of that possibility? What effect will a decline have on costs, and have you built that contingency into the agreed payments?

A leasing arrangement could be upset by a change in the way one operates. A recent example was an organisation, which just over a year after entering into a six-year computer lease, decided to replace it with a different computer, which was to be phased in over three years. This left an expensive unused asset for the last two of these years.

Business changes

A general change in business direction could mean that you have an expensive outsourcing contract for a service you may no longer need. It would be an irony if the outsourced activity, carried out to achieve greater flexibility, could in this case lock you into a routine you no longer required.

Acquisitions and mergers

What happens if you acquire or are acquired? The contract must take account of this possibility, and be capable of renegotiation. It is well documented that several UK building society mergers were called off solely because of the incompatibility of their respective computer and telecommunications technologies.

De-mergers

ICI was the largest recent example of this. A rigid outsourcing contract can inhibit company de-mergers as well as mergers. The very act of outsourcing is itself part of an increasing trend of conglomerates to release locked in shareholder value and downsize.

On the other hand, outsourcing can be a facilitator for structural business change if planned in advance, as in the rationale behind the leading UK financial services organisation, Hoare Govett, outsourcing the operation of its dealing room to Digital. When Hoare Govett split from its parent, which had provided its information technology, the de-merger was facilitated by the outsourcing action. This avoided the difficulties and risks of splitting up this function.

Not properly prequalifying the supplier

Even though you can do all the right things in house, you can still choose the wrong supplier, so the prequalification of the supplier is all important (see Appendix IV). For example, if you want a five-year contract you should choose a large and stable supplier; if you want lowest cost you should ensure that the supplier has economies of scale and many similar customers.

People

A recent report from US consultants Wyatt Co, which did a survey of 531 mainly large companies, revealed the dangers of badly managed downsizing, particularly when staff issues are not handled properly. The study also revealed that more than half of the surveyed companies had refilled positions within a year of eliminating them.

Certain issues need to be addressed before you embark on the outsourcing project.

Assessing the skills inventory

You will need to carry out a skills inventory – what do you have, what should you keep, not keep, what is your right size? These are questions which may be answered only by benchmarking.

During the 1980s and early part of the 1990s a number of European governments were rightly considering ways to reduce public service workforces. Under the circumstances the only practical way to do so was to offer early retirement with generous pensions and lump sums. Most of the recipients ended up in early retirement; a few, however, took the opportunity to start up substantial businesses of their own, doing in the private sector what they were not able to do because of restrictive job descriptions in the public sector. The activities which they adopted were from areas of former employment. State bodies were therefore paying off certain key staff to leave and be successful for themselves, who could, had there been a truly facilitative organisational structure, made their organisations better. They were being paid not to make a better enterprise of their own organisation, but to go off and make money for themselves.

While there may have been no other way for a public service to get rid of excess staff, no private company can afford to embark upon a process which will shed its key staff, or potential key staff. The warning could also be expressed as 'don't throw the baby out with the bath water'. Are there key skills on which you are reliant that are giving you a competitive edge?

Identify these skills and decide how to handle them. Do you keep them in house as part of the supplier management role? Do you look for guarantees that you will have sole access to them? If they are key skills, you must make sure that they are not dispersed within the supplier's organisation and therefore unavailable to you.

As well as identifying which skills to keep, you should decide what new skills you need in house to manage the outsourcing process itself?

Outsourcing is new to most of the people who have to manage an outsourcing relationship for the first time and there is a potential conflict of interest at this interface. Both sides have to recognise and manage that conflict which can come from one side looking to maximise profit margin and the other looking to maximise service.

The supplier can also cause a project to fail. Often the supplier will put in a project manager who will do what project managers do well and that is to manage the tangibles of time, money, resources and so on. This is a particular pitfall of suppliers who are new to outsourcing and one can see it too often in those coming from product backgrounds. Delivering a product or a project is definitely not the same as delivering a service.

Not taking account of people legislation

You should know the legislation for the country you are operating in. In the EU, this is known as the Acquired Rights Directive and in the UK as Transfer of Undertakings (Protection of Employment) Regulations 1981, usually abbreviated to TUPE. You need to understand at the outset of negotiations whether this legislation applies. Both sides run a risk if they are not certain of whether they are bound by legislation. When Procord, a buildings facilities management company spun off from IBM some years ago, took over buildings management for British Gas, they jointly agreed to assume that TUPE applied and constructed a contract that was within the legislation, thus avoiding any retrospective application of the rules as and when they become clearer.

You should consult your own legal advisers about this legislation (see also Appendix III).

Unhappy people will not work

Outsourcing negotiations can rarely be kept totally quiet, and it may be advisable at a certain stage to inform your staff about what is happening. There are always concerns about job security, no matter how much protection is afforded by either a TUPE-type law or the staff contract, such as that under the full employment policies of some companies, particularly those in the public sector.

No matter how small the percentage of people that are affected, *all* of them will be worried about change and about uncertainty. If they worry, they are unhappy, and if they are unhappy they will not be giving 100 per cent to the job at hand. Such a situation will not be in anyone's interests and must be avoided.

Early retirement or redundancy arrangement

The people considerations should begin at the start of discussions about outsourcing, which means early liaison with the human resources department. The work which needs to be carried out includes assessments of core competencies/skills, company philosophies, culture and values, human resources practices, policies and procedures, and the potential 'show-stoppers' as they are known in US slang (the spectacular show stopper when the Swedish management called off the much heralded Renault–Volvo merger is described in Chapter 14).

An outline people transition plan is shown in Appendix II.

Managing the change in relationships

When a service is delivered from in-house, users will take it for granted. Even where there is a service level agreement in place, as there is in some companies with, say, building services, that service is not exposed to all of the commercial realities which exist when it is outsourced.

The changes that outsourcing brings are difficult for both sides to adjust to and need to be understood and managed. One day the relationship is with a colleague, the next it is with a supplier who has commercial motives.

A department of a large organisation, for example, was hived off as a separate company and contracted through a service level agreement to provide a service back to its previous employers.

Overnight the people supplying the service went from being colleagues who were 'on tap' to help others in the organisation to being suppliers who had to be sensitive to the cost of the service they were now contracted to deliver.

As a side issue, but important nevertheless, the suppliers were resented by those who had once been their fellow workers and who now assumed (perhaps wrongly) that they had all become wealthy overnight.

Not involving the users from the outset

Outsourcing is about delivering a service and, irrespective of what it says in the service level agreement, the final arbiters of whether the service is good, bad or indifferent are the users. They are the ones who will make it work or fail. It is therefore important to ensure the users are satisfied. The good contractor will insist on regular satisfaction surveys, particularly in the early stages of a contract, as part of the input to the management reviews of performance.

Not getting people used to each other

Interestingly, Kodak sent its own staff and those of the prospective outsource supplier to an intensive negotiating course to learn these skills. Only when they had completed the course did they start negotiating the details of the contract.

Kodak gave one outsourcing contract to IBM to manage its data centres, one to Digital for management of its network, and a third to Businessland for the management and support of PCs and desktops. It is interesting to note that after three years the IBM contract was perceived by both sides to be successful whereas the Digital contract was in some difficulties. During these three years IBM had employed the same manager for the job, while Digital had put in at least three different senior managers to run their contract. One may draw some conclusions on the importance of a working relationship to the stability of an outsourcing contract.

Some examples of the people experience

In the following examples the people issue at the UK's two largest contracts will be considered.

When the UK Inland Revenue signed a £1 billion-plus, ten-year outsourcing contract with EDS (Electronic Data Systems, the world's largest outsourcing company), and British Aerospace a ten-year contract worth almost £900 million with Computer Sciences, both principals were motivated by expectations of significant cost reductions coming from the rationalisation of staffing levels.

The Inland Revenue Staff Federation (IRSF), the trade union involved with Inland Revenue, was less than happy with the adventure, especially as it had not been allowed to make an internal staff bid.

Clive Brooke, IRSF general secretary, had this to say: 'It is regrettable that the only people who can show they can do the job properly – the staff who do it now – have been prevented from bidding for their own work.

'We do not accept the need for this privatisation and we believe the timetable is being rushed. No one can guarantee the same security and confidentiality of taxpayer information as Revenue staff. Privatisation can only add unnecessary dangers.'

The UK's Labour Party supported this as Michael Meacher MP, shadow minister for the Citizen's Charter, announced: 'Individual tax payers certainly need to be worried. There is a major increase in the risk of snooping on their personal lives.

'Businesses need to be worried. Their most sensitive confidential records could be available to their rivals, at a price of course, as could information on profit projections, how much they pay their employees, their research programmes, their cash-flow projections and other information that could affect their credit worthiness.'

William Waldegrave responded as follows in the House of Commons: 'It is extremely unwise to assume that those in the private sector who own a duty of confidentiality – and who are still covered by the law and the criminal offence of the release of any information – are less likely to behave properly than those in the public sector. Most people in this country work in the private sector. They are as honourable and behave as well as people in the public sector.'

Before their transfer from the Inland Revenue to EDS, managers were reassured by Peter Clough, head of the new Inland Revenue division within EDS and a former RAF engineer, as follows: 'You will be joining a company whose success lies in the strengths and commitment of its people. Many of us, including myself, transferred to EDS from other organisations and understand the concerns you are likely to have experienced during this period of uncertainty. We will be explaining in more detail our approach to the partnership and the transfer arrangements, and we aim to address your concerns.

'But let me make clear from the outset that your terms and conditions of employment, including pensions, will be comparable to those you enjoyed as civil service employees.'

The UK TUPE regulations, which guarantee the rights of employees transferred to a new organisation, give the staff some protection; however, what that is worth will be seen if and when EDS decides to re-engineer delivery of the service it has taken over. Some commentators have speculated on the potential for significant efficiencies when the 2000 staff become part of a commercial enterprise.

In British Aerospace, 1250 staff will transfer to CSC. The fate of other staff is not clear.

BBC management found the potential pitfalls so great that they first rejected the option of outsourcing their financial and administrative workload. According to Bryan Parlett, business manager of bureau services, 'We analysed all the claimed advantages of outsourcing and decided we could do as well, if not better, in house by doing things differently. We put change programmes in place, reduced the number of computer mainframes from five to two, improved the service and achieved savings.'

Only BBC insiders will know the truth, but if these were the real reasons, another pitfall would be to give away rich pickings to outsource suppliers which you could harvest yourself, particularly if you are being exposed to other pitfalls in the process.

Although the option of outsourcing was originally rejected by the BBC, in 1993 a combination of developments, including the necessity to relocate a datacentre and the spread of desktop PCs, meant escalating costs, so information processing was, after all, outsourced to CFM (Computer Facilities Management).

Many of Parlett's fears were confirmed; he found the evaluation process to be both 'trying' and time-consuming, involving in-depth examination and lengthy discussions with potential suppliers. He explained: 'Outsourcing causes major disruption to an organisation and to a lot of its people. You have to devote a lot of time and energy to the evaluation and decision making process.'

This prospect of disruption, coupled with fears about losing control of key functions, are key concerns.

Jane Baker, chief operating officer of the London Stock Exchange during negotiations with Andersen Consulting for the transfer of the information, trading and settlement systems, recognising the sensitivities, advised: 'The supplier must have an established reputation for handling transferred staff who feel aggrieved, absorbing them into the organisation and then swinging them around to feel good about a client who was their employer.'

Apparently the London Stock Exchange was spending over £50 million a year to run and maintain fragile, ageing systems in urgent need of replacement, with annual costs rising by 20 per cent. Outsourcing was part of an ambitious target to reduce the running costs of existing systems to £30 million in five years and to use the savings to build a new trading system.

There was no competitive tendering in the supplier evaluation equation. The process focused on the abilities of both parties to work creatively together. As Baker put it: 'Since we wanted all the savings to come to the Exchange, we recognised we would have to shoulder some of the risk. So we retained the hardware, software, networks and buildings, while Andersen took over the people. Our risk is that we don't have enough resources: Andersen's risk is they don't have enough people.'

Technology

Companies are evolving to give more power to lower levels, more local autonomy, more accountability. These trends, together with emerging technology, will make smart users weigh what they are having to pay for an outsourcing deal against what might be achieved by using their own technology. Deciding whether a company has its own PCs or uses an outsourced service from a large mainframe computer is a prime example of this.

The result of a poor technology decision could be that the centrally provided function becomes inefficient and the customer pays both for a centralised service from the outsource supplier and for allowing the internal users to expand their own internal technology. The same could be true of staff setting up their own lunch service after a catering agreement.

Application development and maintenance

Outsourcing a 'development function', which is where new systems are being developed or programmed, has not been popular to date. It has been seen as giving too great a monopoly to the supplier with too few ways of measuring value for money to the end user of the service.

In IT, similarly, there have been few application development outsourcing successes. This is probably due to the traditional type of outsourcing contract that has used measurements similar to those used for operational outsourcing, such as data centres.

There has been little outsourcing in this area because development is much less tangible than operations and it is typically more strategic to the business. A different approach to the problem is needed as well as a higher level of maturity on both sides. It involves more sharing of risk, more openness in accounting and more trust from both parties, and these have only recently become accepted features of outsourcing relationships.

How to share in the benefits of advances in technology

Different factors will affect the cost profile of outsourcing contracts during their life. Those that are purely people intensive will have a cost profile which rises with inflation and pay settlements, and falls with the improved productivity of those people (including economies of scale).

IT outsourcing contracts, for example, are in part technology sensitive. Everyone knows that the costs of IT are coming down (even though the IT budget keeps going up). If this is a certainty, what is uncertain is the extent to which a contract can take advantage of technology advances (such as new disk storage) over time.

Good contracts will ensure that the company and the out-source supplier share the cost benefits that accrue from exploiting cheaper technology.

Ensuring licences are re-assignable to the vendor

In the case of licensed products such as software and other know-how, suppliers will require that the licence be reassigned to them for their use. Beware – these rights may not be transferable. Find out early if this is the case as you may need to negotiate round the inflexibility of the license holder or remove it from the contract. Planning ahead could and will save a lot of wasted effort.

One company recently received a bad press over its intransigence. It refused to allow a large supplier to use its software, which had been transferred to it as part of a huge outsourcing contract from a government department of a European state. Unless negotiations succeed, major programme redevelopment will have to be undertaken.

Do not give away the strategy

If development is strategic rather than to do with tactical or day-to-day operations, then the development of the strategy itself is core to the business. Of all the functions which can be candidates for outsourcing this must be the one to keep in-house.

Plan for possible disasters

If your process is critical to the business, it is still critical when run by an outsource supplier. Do not assume that the outsource suppliers are taking the same view. They may not want to offer a disaster standby facility unless it is explicitly covered (and priced) in the contract. Out of 'site' out of mind could be a good phrase for this pitfall.

Lessons and conclusions

1   Understand the business model of your outsource suppliers. Where will they make money? Where will they achieve the

economies of scale? Where can they (and only they) achieve efficiencies that you cannot get yourself?

2   Understand where they will make savings. What will they cut out? Were there any points on which they were inflexible during negotiations? (Was everything negotiable at a price?) Remember the typical supplier model:
   - Supplier invests (in set up, capital, people etc.) for two to three years.
   - Supplier makes profit in years 3 to n.

3   There will be costs to establish the outsourcing service. Make sure these are quoted separately. Do not let it be an opportunity for the outsource supplier to charge premium prices for commodity services.

4   Before contracting, discuss with the outsource supplier as many ways in which business requirements might change as possible. Agree how to handle those that just may possibly come about, even if there is a 'catch-all' clause in the contract.

5   In the early stages of contract negotiation, keep checking and testing the assumptions you have both made and do this at regular intervals. How do you plan to operate these two systems in parallel during a transition? Whose staff/premises will be used?

6   Outsourcing contracts have to be flexible. Changes should be able to be initiated by both sides for the contract to be really workable.

7   The contract needs to motivate *both* sides to deliver improved technology efficiencies and cost-effectiveness to the business.

8   Avoid pitfalls by:
   - communicating what is being done
   - keeping on top of the delivery of the service – it is a two-way process
   - conducting user satisfaction surveys that form part of the management review process.

Pitfall checklist

Check that all the following have been taken account of:

1 loss of control
2 security risks
3 threats to confidentiality
4 quality/expertise of outsource supplier
5 escalation of costs
6 potential of removal of activity from end customer, i.e. breaking contact between customer and developer
7 loss of expertise within company
8 change in commitment/financial stability of outsource supplier
9 business and technology change during the lifetime of a contract (product change also?)
10 environmental changes, for example enlargement of European Union, NAFTA, GATT
11 bringing it back in-house
12 mismatch of customer–supplier motivations/skills.

Pitfalls for the bidder

As well as the principal, the bidder may also be exposed to pitfalls.

In 1994 Digital decided that for the time being it would not bid for any more large outsourcing contracts following its failure to obtain large projects at British Aerospace and the Inland Revenue. The reason was that it had cost millions to fund the bids and it was not prepared to risk such investment if it had to compete with no certainty of obtaining the business.

Digital UK's managing director, Chris Conway, was quoted in the media as saying, 'Digital is not very well positioned either to compete for or run a mammoth outsourcing task such as that sought by the Inland Revenue.

'In addition, a successful bid requires an enormous upfront investment – millions of dollars. I'm not prepared to make such an investment without a greater certainty of success.'

The two jobs in question were worth a staggering £2 billion. It was no comfort either that IBM, with the help of an outsourcing partner, was a successful bidder for half of the prize. Even with Barclays Bank and Logica as partners, Digital did not make the shortlist.

'Until we have established a proven track record of successful projects on a smaller scale, we are not likely to persuade the market of our competence in this arena,' said Conway.

Considerations before deciding to outsource

Here is a list of areas to consider before outsourcing an information technology department:

- the location of the service
- adequate security arrangements
- service and capacity availability
- access to advanced technology
- migration possibilities to more advanced systems
- ability to manage to and report on Service Level Agreement
- software support
- contingency plans in place
- recovery from disaster
- network support and integration
- relationship with PTTs (national telecom companies – post, telegraph and telecommunications)
- PC user support
- help desk for business and PC applications
- training of users, first line support, systems administrators.

What is interesting about the above is that it can be applied to many other functions. Here is a catering version:

- the location of the service
- adequate security arrangements
- service and capacity availability
- quality of service

- access to advanced technology
- migration possibilities to more advanced systems
- ability to manage to and report on Service Level Agreement
- specialist dietary support
- contingency plans in place
- recovery from disaster
- relationship with suppliers
- staff advice on dietary issues.

Summary

Inefficient handling of the project and business and technology changes can cause difficulties and even lead to the failure of the project. The biggest danger, however, is that the people issue will not be dealt with properly.

The Wyatt study revealed that more than half of the surveyed companies had refilled positions within a year of eliminating them, while the UK press has been full of stories about difficulties with staff and unions in the UK Market Testing Programme. The problem is not just how you can pass staff over to a supplier, but how you can avoid losing your most skilled staff or even your core skills.

5 What can be outsourced – and what can't

A study by Input, the US research company, literature from the UK government's Market Testing Programme, IBM and other companies all give us useful information on what can be outsourced and what may not be. This information is summarised below and could form a basic guide to selecting processes for the outsourcing project.

What can be outsourced

Traditional services

An outstanding example of a company involved in a high degree of outsourcing is a book publisher. A modern book publisher may outsource all routine editing, design and artwork, printing, packaging and delivery. This is, of course, all on top of the main material outsourced – the text from writers.

The publisher is not likely to outsource core competencies. These are the original scrutiny and editing of scripts, the management of authors, strategic market assessment and product selection and, perhaps, marketing itself, although even the last it seems is being outsourced by some.

What the publisher achieves by outsourcing so much can be a lesson for all companies. Outside experts are allowed to suggest marketable products, which is part of the research and development function, other outside experts can then design and develop the products, which more outsiders can produce and package.

That huge burden of manufacturing, printing, is also outsourced, leaving the publisher the time and energy to concentrate on the core competencies of dealing with authors and markets.

Although the publisher may be the quintessential outsourcer, there are a number of functions which have been outsourced for generations. Principal amongst these are accountancy – particularly auditing – legal services, transport, printing and advertising. These have been joined in recent decades by such services as security, canteen, public relations, data processing, management consultancy, landscaping, maintenance, electronic communications and courier services. Now even the most central processes are being outsourced.

The functions which have been traditionally outsourced can be summarised as follows:

- sub-supply of materials and components
- general services (catering, landscaping, security)
- information technology
- consultancy and training.

New opportunities

In the current environment where increasingly whole processes formerly carried on in-house are being outsourced, the extent of outsourcing may be explained in the following terms:

- the traditional services
- current and new services
- core competencies
- projects, such as new developments and directions.

The traditional services are listed above. The current and new services are the whole business process which may include administration and information processing, buildings facilities management covering both buildings and a wide range of related services, new product development, design, and research and development.

The core competencies would never be outsourced by some companies. Glaxo UK sees the development of new drugs as its core competency. Hewlett Packard talks of not outsourcing its core development work and manufacture. There seems little that IBM would not outsource (see page 179).

The management of projects is ideal for outsourcing and is a huge area of opportunity for suppliers, especially consultants. These projects can range from construction to the implementation of new systems.

The activities of suppliers

The activities of outsource suppliers, such as Merchant Gardner (see Chapter 13) and buildings facilities management providers (see Chapter 11) show that a process which has been going on between world class manufacturers and their suppliers is now taking place in the outsourcing activity: more and more work is going to fewer and fewer suppliers. Building service suppliers are expanding into a huge range of services from security to running the courier service and catering companies are expanding from the kitchen to landscaping.

The prime driver for this process of expansion appears to be the marketing of the suppliers who are smart enough to see the opportunities and who realise that they cannot stand still in a world where business is evolving and re-engineering itself.

Niche expertise

Tom Peters is supposed to have first advised that you should do what you do best and outsource the rest, so perhaps a simpler description of the core competency not to be outsourced is that which you do best, which you need to keep also as a strategic advantage. This is another reason for the value of today's niche markets, the existence of which may owe more to niche expertise than niche demand. Indeed, niche expertise is the key to today's successful enterprises at the smaller end of the scale, as is demonstrated by the healthy markets which continue for niche consultants – not to mention business book writers.

Where the niche expertise is the treasure for the very small enterprises, it provides the specialised activity which forms the main platform for growth for the flourishing facilities management suppliers, the main platforms having been computing, catering, buildings management and security.

And this raises an interesting question. Who were the traditional suppliers, already with access to many companies, who missed out on the opportunities to expand their supply of services to those customers.

The emergence of new specialist suppliers

The main area to fail must be the accounting profession, with the exception of those few such as Andersen who had already spun off successful management consulting companies. The fact that consultants such as Andersen Consulting are now *managing* operating departments for their customers, as distinct from giving advice, is a reflection of the extent of the change and an example of the threat to traditional accountants.

What have accountants missed out on? They missed computing in the first instance, and allowed a whole profession of information technologists to emerge. By the time they had caught up with the emergence of computing, they had also completely missed the quality revolution and are now also missing the environmental revolution. The true extent of what they have lost is seen in the fact that both the quality and environmental management standards involve auditing, which is now carried out by engineers. The latest practice of developing general management standards and related generic documentation will put the very reason for the existence of accountants to the test.

Printers and packaging companies have also failed to take advantage of the outsourcing trend. Many fell by the wayside as manufacturers began to do more business with fewer suppliers, giving all their printing to one printer for example. Some printers, offered the stationery business also by their customers, refused it and lost all the business. Those print and packaging people able to stay the course who have ended up as the single supplier have not in any significant numbers been able to expand their business beyond the traditional range. New opportunities are now opening up, if they see them, in the regulations for packaging waste, which could lead to other environmental management services.

Solicitors also performed badly. They had many opportunities to help companies to develop control systems for the burgeoning regulatory environment but they left it to struggling consultants, not at all familiar with this difficult terrain, to develop a new niche market. This was worse than accountants losing computing and quality as legal service suppliers were losing legal services. Again there are some notable exceptions (see the Masons contribution in Appendix III).

Advertising companies have not done so well, despite their established positions, nor have public relations consultants. They appear to be unaware of the growing amount of technical writing being carried out by their technical customers, particularly manufacturers. This was simply asking to be outsourced to advertising and PR agencies who were already supplying related products and services, but, instead, it either stayed in house or went to new specialists who saw the niche and seized the opportunity. Ordinary freelance journalists also missed out on this huge technical writing market, preferring to compete with each other in an over supplied general market than to consider such mundane business.

Functions which companies are most likely to outsource

The Input study (see Chapter 10) contains revealing remarks about the kinds of operation that companies are more likely to outsource, which is information of strategic importance to potential suppliers. They found these operations were labour intensive and were those which showed considerable peaks and troughs of activity. In addition, companies are more likely to outsource activities which they perceive to be commonplace and not unique to their own organisations.

These operations can be compared with the functions the British government in its Market Testing Programme (see Chapter 8) believes can be more easily outsourced. These are:

- those which are resource intensive – running cost or capital investment
- relatively discrete areas
- specialist and other support services
- those with fluctuating work patterns in loading and throughput
- those subject to a quickly changing market and one where it is costly to recruit, train and retain staff
- those with a rapidly changing technology requiring expensive investment.

Not listed is Input's 'those which are commonplace and not unique to their own organizations'.

What not to outsource

Although every function listed below may have been successfully outsourced by someone somewhere, you should think carefully before outsourcing the following:

- Management of strategic planning
- Management of finances
- Management of management consultancy
- Control of suppliers
- Quality and environmental management
- The supervision of the meeting of market and regulatory requirements, such as
  - product liability
  - misleading advertising
  - quality

 – environmental regulations
 – staff health and safety
 – public safety
 – product/service safety.

All of the regulatory requirements carry risks of both corporate and personal liability.

A simple way to look at the decision may be in the following table:

Value/nature	*Decision*
Strategic	Keep in-house
Highly profitable	Keep in-house
Routine/support	Outsource

The above list does not take into account the policy of IBM Europe (see Chapter 17). As IBM is probably prepared to outsource more functions than any other company, the elements which IBM will not outsource (at least for now) are listed separately. They are those that:

- provide management and direction
- maintain competence and control
- differentiate IBM from its competitors
- sustain IBM's uniqueness.

Summary

One of the first steps in the outsourcing project, and perhaps the most important, is selecting the processes which might be outsourced. It is useful therefore to have a list of the criteria for deciding what are likely areas for outsourcing and what are not. The findings used here are very straightforward, and few will

have difficulty in establishing what processes within a company
are:

- resource intensive
- in relatively discrete areas
- using specialist and other support services
- with fluctuating work patterns in loading and throughput
- subject to a quickly changing market – where it is costly
  to recruit, train and retain staff, and where there is rapidly
  changing technology requiring expensive investment

Nor will you have difficulty establishing those processes which
are commonplace and not unique to your own organisation.

Conversely, you will be able to establish the processes not
amenable to outsourcing, by looking at those which involve:

- strategy
- corporate finance
- control of suppliers
- quality
- environmental standards
- safety
- the meeting of market and regulatory requirements
- the provision of management and direction
- the maintenance of competence and control
- the differentiation from competitors
- the sustaining of one's uniqueness.

6 Is outsourcing a one-way street?

You may have outsourced a vital function to what appeared to be a competent and caring provider, only to find neither competence nor care, but instead that you have made a big mistake. The first question you will ask is whether you are now locked into an agreement from which you cannot extricate yourself for years, or whether you have included opt out clauses.

The initial enthusiasm for acquiring a partner may mean you neglect to ensure that you can terminate the deal, but you must remember that even the best laid plans may come to grief, especially where personnel in the supplier change.

The questions and lessons

These are the main questions which must be asked and answered if you are to avoid going down a one-way street:

- Can you recover back in-house at end of contract?
- What contingencies need planning for?
- Have you assessed the risks?

- What requirements should you impose on your suppliers?
- Have you retained key skills to 're-start' the function?
- Can you change suppliers if you need to?

Renegotiating or terminating a contract after signing it is not simple and the last thing any manager who has just finalised an agreement for outsourcing needs is a visit to court. Even a principal as powerful as the UK's Inland Revenue has run into legal problems trying to pass software to its new outsource supplier.

In that initial enthusiasm for tenders and negotiations, it can appear to be over pessimistic to consider how to terminate your outsourcing deal – after all where is the trust, the true partnership? But it can be easy to forget that a meticulously negotiated contract could be more of a burden than a blessing in the years to come.

Most partners do not have this problem and results can be gauged by the numbers who do renew contracts at the end of contract term, and by the even fewer who decide to get out early. However, as the market matures and more contracts come up for renewal, some changeovers are inevitable.

One of the concerns of clients is loss of control and being locked in, according to Graham Jump, senior consultants at Coopers and Lybrand and recently appointed chairman of the CSSA (Computing Services and Software Association) FM (facilities management) special interest group. 'The worry is that the supplier may hold too many trump cards at the contract renewal point, making it far too difficult to change to another supplier. Clients don't want to feel coerced into continuing with a provider.'

As a result the CSSA's code of conduct for facilities management suppliers says that they should provide 'all reasonable assistance' when the contract terminates to transfer the provision of the services back to the client, or to another third party. The supplier is also responsible for commencing contract renewal negotiations in sufficient time to enable the user, if necessary, to make alternative arrangements.

It is not, however, wise to rely solely on the good intentions of suppliers. Graham Jump puts the onus on to users to think and plan ahead when writing the contract. 'You need to try and look into the future as much as possible and consider the stage when the contract ends. The more things you can attempt to predict, the better.'

It is essential to make sure the contract covers all eventualities, says the CSSA code, especially when the supplier's premises, hardware and software are being shared with other clients.

Justifying termination

The company Consultancy OTR, in a recent report on the out-sourcing market, emphasises the importance of defining situations that justify termination or renegotiation such as the failure to meet set service level agreements, or the supplier being taken over or going bankrupt.

Torfaen Borough Council, for instance, signed a six-year contract with Municipal Mutual Computing (MMC) in early 1992 to look after its computing centre in Pontypool. However, in October 1992 MMC were unable to continue with the contract because of change in corporate ownership. 'Fortunately we had a unique clause in our contract that if there was any change of majority shareholder, the council would have the immediate option to terminate the contract or renegotiate,' says Gwyn James, borough treasurer. Torfaen exercised that right and chose Telecom Capita to take over the job.

Gwyn James added: 'We were aware that MMC could be sold off and that we might not have liked our new partner, so we included this get-out clause in the contract.'

Torfaen also considered its own future. 'We were worried about local government reorganisation scheduled for 1994–96 and the possibility of our going out of existence,' says James. 'We needed our own get-out clause; otherwise we'd be in trouble if the FM company did not wish to terminate.'

Users should also try to anticipate situations which might require renegotiating the contract. There may be a reduction in requirements as a result of centralisation, company reorganisation or government legislation. Alternatively, new systems or increased business volumes may lead to an increased service need.

The lessons of contract catering

If a company is running its own catering operation, and is finding it impossible to meet service demands out of its staff resources, because of location perhaps, will an outside supplier be any more successful at finding adequate staff who are properly trained and motivated for this sensitive service?

Principals should be aware that the handing out of facilities to contract catering companies may require a demonstration from the caterer that subcontractors with proven skills and track records will be used. With possible contract terms of five years, companies need to know who else is being invited in to feed staff.

Catering can also be used as a benchmark against which to assess what regulations or standards, and what performance measurements, need to be set for many other activities. First on the list in catering must come hygiene and microbiological control. The top supermarkets and hotels can demonstrate third party accreditation of best codes of practice, so contract caterers should be able to do this also. The ISO 9000 Services Standard is a good start, as will be a number of hygiene assessment schemes. Large supermarkets employ rigorous hygiene training programmes. Does your prospective contract caterer?

The health and safety regulations, compulsory for all, are another benchmark. How well does the caterer know them? Where is the certification? Is it supplied by a health inspector, or a third party food hygiene inspectorate? Are the regulations also controlled under an environmental management system such as BS 7750?

Above all, contract catering, so much now taken for granted, is an example of how management must be constantly vigilant to potential exposure from the shortcomings of suppliers or sub-contractors. What is the legal position if staff contract salmonella or suffer other food poisoning? Are they indemnified in the contract against such occurrences?

Apart from the legal issues, service and staff morale issues need to be considered. If the contract caterer has grown so large over the years that you are just one of many clients and service levels are falling, there is a good case for continually reviewing service levels and keeping the possibility of changing to a smaller supplier in mind. It is also easy for contract caterers to employ people who may have low standards or be low paid. There is a useful and easy to use measuring device – staff. Are staff happy with the service? Are they using the facility or going down to the local café? Can you bring visitors to your canteen? Do you eat there yourself?

There is a similarity here between outsourcing the mainframe computer department and then finding staff doing all the work on their PCs and bringing in a contract caterer and discovering the staff are relocating to the local pub.

Contract catering may be the best benchmark for long-established and profitable outsourced activities. A key question is whether your outsource suppliers have themselves reached a size and a 'level of paralysis' where they also need a shake up and more competition?

Summary

Ask the questions before and not when it is too late. Plan for recovery at any stage of the contract including at its termination. Think out the contingencies. Fully assess the risks. Know the requirements which should be imposed on your suppliers. Keep key skills in case you have to re-start the function.

7 Getting started

This chapter discusses some of the major issues which need consideration when getting a project started and providing a measure of control (see also Appendix IV for a working methodology).

How do you begin?

Checklist for the main project steps

1   Getting the commitment
2   Selection of project leader
3   Devising the detailed methodology
4   Drawing up the project plan
5   Creating the project team
6   Implementation of the assessment study
7   Reporting of findings/proposal (if necessary)
8   Selection/planning of the specific outsource project(s)
9   Selecting the providers (including tendering)
10 Passing over control to external controller.

Details of each step

1   Getting the commitment

This is a much more difficult matter than any previous management decision to adopt a new technology, new product line or implement a management system to a new standard, as this decision is based not just simply on an analysis of whether a specific function might be hived off to outsiders, but what functions across the enterprise, including perhaps your own, should be hived off.

Apart from the obvious human relations implications for the staff involved, there are the personal and political implications for the senior managers who are making the decision in the first instance.

Where obtaining the commitment to a project, such as the implementation of a new management standard, had the perceived good of all at stake in the past, this decision is now fraught with threatening implications for many, possibly even for the senior executive examining the question.

The board should be motivated by its responsibilities to the shareholders and is the least likely group to be hoping for a 'golden parachute'. Under the board, commitment should come from either a CEO or a senior management team involved with the decision. These people will be protected from an unfavourable outcome of the deliberations as they will have to be told what their own job will be after the project. Alternatively, there is a strong case for using outsiders.

It will still be difficult to get the process under way unless a sponsor emerges in the form of a 'courageous' manager to raise the issue with the CEO. It can also be raised by the agreement of several managers at a senior management committee meeting. At this point the highly political decision of who will take charge of the project will emerge.

Possible sources of inspiration for the project include: CEO, senior manager, management committee, the board, proposal from a potential provider, proposal from consultant.

Once the commitment has been made, the project team can be drawn up.

2   Selection of project leader

No hard or fast rules can be laid down as the CEO will probably pick the best person available, but helpful backgrounds would include: systems engineering, business process re-engineering, implementation of new ISO 9000 or environment management systems, materials management and purchasing (although that last position on its own may not be senior enough and certainly will not be suitable if the incumbent is still at the pre-partnership stage with suppliers). Also suitable would be an outside consultant, or someone working in a core competency.

If clear core competencies which will not be outsourced have been formally identified at this stage, the leader of the project team may be selected from one of these competencies.

On the other hand, the decision may be made to use an outside consultant. However, although some consultants may be experienced at business process re-engineering and many have had experience of re-organisation, it may be difficult to identify a consultant who has any knowledge or experience of a structured approach to the outsourcing project.

3   Devising the detailed methodology

The main elements in the methodology are laid out in Appendix IV. They include factor selection, costing the options, appraising the potential benefits, assessment of suppliers, and assessing risks and opt outs. You should attempt to evaluate the potential benefits of:

- freeing managers for more effective work
- access to the latest technology/market data/information
- faster deployment of new developments and application
- better or re-engineered processes
- better customer satisfaction.

4   Drawing up the project plan

A new ISO standard on this subject is available in draft form: *ISO 9004–6 Quality management and quality system elements – Part 6: Guidelines to quality in project management.*

A reasonable plan would encompass:

- detailed project plan
- assignment of tasks
- report of initial findings
- selection/planning of the specific outsourcing projects(s).

5   Creating the project team

The selection of project leader, who should report to the CEO, is by far the most important step in creating the project team. It would be useful for the team members to have skills in systems engineering, design engineering (or new product development), marketing or PR, materials management/purchasing and finance. An outside management consultant, reporting to the team leader could make a contribution.

The benefit of including marketing/PR people in the team is that they know what the customer wants, and usually also know why the customer is not getting it, for example, they will be the first to know what operating departments are not delivering the goods on time and to the right specification, or not giving the required level of service.

6   Implementation of the assessment study

This is the point where the project could die, particularly if the board sits on the findings of the assessment and the project team fades away. The team leader should be authorised from the beginning to continue with the project right up to the selection of the potential providers and tendering.

7   Reporting of findings/proposal

IBM provides a good example of the importance of bringing a well presented case to the board (see Chapter 17). The report writer should be skilled, while the hard copy report should be supported by an overhead presentation.

8   Selection/planning of the specific outsourcing project(s)

The selection/planning will depend on what authority has been given to the team. Do they come back for approval for each specific project or can they 'market test' before looking for approval to outsource? The ease with which this is done will reflect both the need and commitment of the company to outsource.

9 Selecting the providers

Once a methodology such as that in Appendix IV has been followed and attention paid to both pitfalls and the legal issues, the selection of a partner can be made.

10 Passing over control to external controller

After the rest of the process has been carried out, passing over control to an external controller will be a matter of routine.

Other elements to be considered

Amongst the elements which need to be considered when both selecting factors for analysis and evaluating potential benefits are the following:

More efficient release management
This could have little potential in some companies but enormous potential in others. Many senior managers and staff members are constrained by their job descriptions. The flattening of organisational structures and the elimination of buffers have been reducing this constraint, but a truly radical approach could yield substantial results. For example, is it possible that the head of design could move to marketing, or the marketing director to design?

One way of evaluating this potential would be to embark on a programme of cross training/familiarisation which allows people to get experience of each function and to request suggestions and ideas.

Unfortunately this area is also fraught with potential staff relations conflicts and opportunities for destructive power politics. Unless the exercise can be agreed in a friendly and democratic way by all concerned, it might be better to hand it over to an outside consultant who will interview people in confidence and report to the head of the project or to the CEO.

Access to latest technology/market/information

This is an excellent heading under which to re-assess the manning of core competencies. Although research and development might seem to be an essential core competency, it is exactly through a function such as outsourced R & D that a company might acquire, or get information on, the latest technologies by dealing with a skilled provider who is operating at the leading edge. There are risks, of course, but this could be a chance to plug into a font of potentiality and creativity.

The same expert in the latest technology will also be a potential source of knowledge of the market because new technologies tend to transcend traditional market borderlines and open up new ones. For example, the writers of business or scientific books are providing both texts and market information.

The risk of creating partnerships with technologists is that they in turn will have other customers, and this is where the trade off between confidentiality and access to new ideas needs to be evaluated. But remember the legal warnings in Chapter 3 and Appendix III.

Information itself is strategic, and the providers may by nature of their very discipline (for example, research) have the time, facilities and expertise to continuously monitor information sources, for example marketing possibilities in the European Union, the implications of GATT or of NAFTA.

Faster deployment of new development/applications

The European automotive manufacturing industry outsources the manufacture of new ECUs (electronic control units) from electronics components manufacturers already experienced in making *structurally similar* components for the computer industry (see Chapter 14). This is a good example of how much quicker it is to embrace and implement a new electronic control device in your own product (automobile) if you can get it from someone already making similar components for other products.

Better re-engineered process

The re-engineering process can be carried out either before or after an outsourcing contract, but if done after, the supplier may reap all the rewards in increased profits.

One big result of a re-engineered process may be better customer satisfaction from a better process.

Here are some of the 'must haves' in the selection criteria for potential providers.

Company size and stability

Big is not necessarily good, but one thing you want to avoid is the nasty surprise one morning of finding that the supplier no longer exists. The partner must be there during the life of the contract.

An important question is how much of the supplier's capacity will you be taking up, not just at the beginning but in two or three years' time. Over 40–50 per cent of that capacity is probably unhealthy. Even the largest customers take up only a part of EDS's capacity. In a recent case where a large telecoms company wanted to outsource an application development division, an important consideration was how quickly the supplier could ensure that more of its output was for other customers by the end of a five-year period. This is a clear case of the customer not wanting to provide most of the supplier's business, although this by no means applies for all functions; a specialist supplier with most capacity available could be attractive in cases such as R & D.

Commitment to the business

Outsource suppliers are in the business of making a profit, not being philanthropic. Their levels of commitment can vary, as can their underlying, or strategic, motivations. You should ascertain whether your proposed supplier really understands what it means to deliver the required service? For example, if the supplier does not have the pricing quite right, it may be tempting to reduce the level of service until it becomes unsatisfactory.

Signs that suppliers are committed include their having existing customers who will speak highly of the service, and being clear on the process for resolving disputes. Is the relationship or the service level agreement the more important? Are their senior management committed? Is the fact that they are in the service business written into their vision, their strategy, their business goals, their mission?

Flexibility of contract
Flexibility is necessary when contracting for the service in the first place, and when taking care of change during the life of the contract.

Contracting for the service
Do suppliers treat the service like a product and offer a fixed contract only, or do they acknowledge that, in reality, each contract has to be different? Most contracts are different and the diversity may be increasing. Flexibility can be tested by examining *what* is being outsourced, for *how long*, what are the *business arrangements* (joint venture, partnership), how it is *financed*, *where* will the service be delivered from (one's own location, the supplier's). Are *people* or other *assets* transferred as part of the arrangement? How much *risk* are they prepared to share and how much *certainty* do they want that they will get their fees?

So, how flexible is the supplier in setting up the initial contract? A good example was Digital's arrangement with Quotron, where the terms of the contract included payment based on Quotron's success in selling their specialised foreign exchange trading system to banks worldwide.

Flexibility during the contract
The inflexibility of outsourcing contracts to allow for change is a common problem. Just about everything in a business – plus a few things which were never even thought of at the outset – can change. You cannot try to predict them all, you can only predict that anything can, and often will, change.

This has many implications. What happens if business volumes double, or halve? How will both partners make sure that they are not locked in to inordinately high costs, and how can the principal make sure that the supplier can still make a profit? What happens if one wants to change systems? If you have outsourced your applications development function, have you effectively given the outsourcer control of your future application development? If so, you must make sure that it cannot apply monopolistic pricing, so build in a value for money test.

What is the outsource supplier bringing to the party?

You need to be clear about what you are asking the supplier to add to, or improve upon, in the service.

If you are aiming to move capital equipment off your balance sheet and on to someone else's and lease it back, the supplier will need financing and operations skills.

Similarly, if you are looking for cheaper processing of operations, you will want suppliers who can bring economies of scale.

If lack of skills or technology is stopping you getting a product on to the market in a competitive way, this is what the outsource should be achieving.

Knowledge of the industry and your business?

How well is the service to be outsourced supporting the business strategy? Is it critical? Is it merely treated as a utility? Is it effective as well as being efficient? Does it really support the business processes?

Research on information technology has shown that there are about twenty applications unique to each industry sector. These applications can determine the performance of companies within the sector, so that getting them right, whether in house or from an outsource, is of paramount importance. Outsource providers must add value to these, not just provide the same service as that from in house. The EDS performance in healthcare and that of Perot in car rental are two examples of value added by suppliers.

When the General Dynamics Corporation and Computer Sciences Corporation (CSC) signed what is still the largest outsourcing contract to date, worth $3 billion over 10 years, knowledge of the industry certainly figured. CSC had started out in the defence industry and knew it better than most. They were aware, for example, of the regulations and had already built many of the applications, so they were well ahead on the learning curve – a position that would have been expensive and time consuming for others to achieve.

Knowing what you want

Companies will have to get used to specifying exactly what they want to outsource in language such as, 'I need a billing system that gets my invoices out by 4 pm on Fridays and gives me a two-second response time to customer enquiries', or 'My hospital wants an information support system that gives me access from any terminal to all patient history, current treatments and recommended medical procedures for this patient'.

Local government is already saying, 'I want the most cost effective way of collecting local taxes, cleaning streets, collecting parking fines, and maintaining schools and leisure centres.' EDS beat others to run the UK Driver and Vehicle Licensing Authority because in effect they said, 'We will deliver you an effective and efficient licensing system, not just computing.'

Pre-qualifying the supplier

You want	You should check that the supplier
A five-year contract	is large, has stable ownership/shareholding (any reasons for instability?) and is committed to outsourcing
Cash injection	has deep pockets and is financially sound
Lowest cost	has many similar customers (i.e. can achieve the economies of scale)
Access to new skills	has the skills, keeps its people up to date in new technologies/techniques, and that you have ready access to these skills.
People sensitivity	will treat your staff with sensitivity (What pay and conditions? What is the attrition rate? Are its staff happy? What has been the experience of others? Will your people be 'lost in transit?')

Coverage

Increasing globalisation means that more and more organisations are operating pan-nationally, whether it is Coca Cola who need to support a bottling plant in Columbia, McDonalds opening an outlet in Moscow, or Citicorp offering a banking service 24 hours a day around the globe. In contrast with this trend, most outsourced service providers are still nationally based. This is appropriate for a local service but, if you are trying to satisfy a multinational demand, the partners have to have that capacity.

Size of company and cultural fit

Does the proposed partner 'feel' right? Is one going to overly dominate the other? Do your people and their people work well together? Have you tried it yet? Do they speak the same business language? Have you worked together before? Did it work? Were you pleased? Did the two managements get on together?

Staff and benefits

Outsourcing is a way of breaking organisational bottlenecks, such as those where the organisation, entrenched positions, or 'turf', can be barriers to change or improved efficiency. So will the supplier take on your staff? What will happen to them (see page 48)?

The European Union's legislation and provisions such as TUPE in the UK place certain responsibilities on suppliers who take over staff, but you must think about more than just the statutory requirements. Will they be scattered around the outsourced organisation? Will you need access to specific people? What if you want to bring the operation back in house? Can the key people be identified? What career opportunities will be offered to your former staff?

Other services

If outsourcing part or all of a function is an early step in re-engineering the business processes, would it be useful if the outsource supplier had other capabilities also that you might need to use at some stage in the future?

Confidentiality
Guarantees are all very well, but be satisfied that the outsource supplier has the right attitude to security and confidentiality of information.

Relationship with third parties
Outsource suppliers are taking higher levels of responsibility. As they do so, they are subcontracting more to third parties and relying on them to provide services or products.

Make sure that the outsource supplier has the right relationships. For example, Perot stated that between 60 and 70 per cent of their contracts with Europcar and East Midlands Electricity would be subcontracted to others. Perot can buy in the commodity services and focus on where they will add value. They saw data centre operations as a commodity to be priced accordingly. On the other hand, one software supplier refused to allow its products to be continued to be used after an outsourcing contract attempted to pass hardware and software to the new supplier, which had the effect of unpredicted changes, of delays and of additional cost.

A common sense approach to the proposed supplier
The following basic questions should also be considered:

- Can some existing supplier with whom you already have a satisfactory outsourcing relationship be considered for this contract? You may have already combined several sources of component and service in a related area in one supplier.
- Is there a qualified employee who may want to set up in a premises outside the plant to be paid on invoice rather than by payroll?
- Can the new provider meet the requirements of your operating regime, such as the need to participate in similar systems of production, communication and even management? For example, if you have a *kanban*, sell one–make one system, can the supplier respond to market demands at the same time as you do?

- Can the supplier share the same electronic marketing network, EDI?
- Is the supplier ISO 9000 certified?
- Do you require the supplier to operate some focused plants – that is whole production lines or even a factory dedicated to your needs? But bear in mind that the supplier should not be completely dependent on you.

Supplier's basic management and personal requirements
- Supplier's attitude.
- Quality of written communications – the quality of the communication and the device (piece of paper perhaps) used for the communication reveal much about the attitude of the communicator.
- Badly thought out questions, or overstatements.
- General presentation, from dress to manners to communications.
- Response – how is the telephone answered?
- Is the supplier interested in responding to your need or trying to sell you something else? This includes so-called inventions and new ideas, some of which may fall into the category known as 'the solution seeking a problem'.

Summary

Outsourcing is a project of prime importance so an organisation must be put in place, plans made and a detailed methodology employed. This chapter and the step-by-step methodology in Appendix IV, together with the checklists in Appendices II and III on the people issues and legal precautions, will help the reader in planning and managing the outsourcing project.

PART II
OUTSOURCING IN ACTION

Introduction to Part II

Part I has discussed the outsourcing process; Part II will examine specific sectors and individual companies. The results of recent studies, including those of PA, Input Corporation and Technology Forecasters Inc., are included as well as valuable and interesting material from companies such as IBM, Gardner Merchant, SCI Systems Inc., Digital, the Lane Group and Body Shop.

Companies from quite different disciplines and backgrounds are now converging in what they can offer. It seems hard to believe at first that one company offering catering, another property management and a third information technology could ever converge and compete, but that is what is happening. A look at the Gardner Merchant list of services demonstrates that contract caterers are no longer simply feeding people.

The Body Shop, dealing with a number of current management issues in its alliance with the Lane Group, is outsourcing at its most sophisticated level. It encompasses the securing of quality and service requirements, and at the same time the implementation of a mechanism for securing environmentally sound transport and delivery by a company determined to protect its environmental probity.

Outsourcing in different sectors

The process of outsourcing is going on in manufacturing companies, in services and in government. It is also sweeping the
financial sector. We now look at different sectors.

Government and the public service

In the public sector, the British government's Market Testing Programme is the outstanding example of outsourcing (see Chapter
8) and is regarded as a benchmark by other governments.

Other countries such as Malaysia had already shown what this
process, which is also regarded as 'privatisation', can do to benefit
an economy and reduce national debt. One immediate effect in
Malaysia was that state enterprises which were losing money and
were a drain on the economy went into profit after being hived
off to private industry. While whole companies and state bodies
are being privatised in the UK, much outsourcing of specific functions is also taking place.

Large multinational corporations

Most large multinational corporations are doing some outsourcing, while many have big programmes linked with re-engineering
and downsizing. The benchmark in the private sector is the outsourcing done by IBM Europe (see Chapter 17).

Large IT users

Until recently, to many people outsourcing meant information
technology only, and for the good reason that this was the biggest
outsourcing area (see Chapter 9 and Chapter 18 which discusses
the experience of Digital).

It appears that over 70 per cent of companies already outsource
some IT services or are considering doing so. This percentage has
increased considerably over the past few years. Digital operates
Quotron's network worldwide, while BT's Syncordia will manage
Glaxo's private network across the US, UK and Canada. Man-
power runs IBM Havant's UK national call management centre
with 100 staff handling 27 000 calls a week.

Electronics contract manufacturing

Contract manufacturing involves huge business being outsourced by computer and all other electronics manufacturers from small, medium-sized and even large suppliers. It may also be called the outside assembly business. Perhaps the best known outsourced device is the PCB (printed circuit board) but all kinds of component and service are outsourced from product development to full volume production.

This business has become very difficult to define because large OEMs, who formerly were seekers of efficiencies through outsourcing and subcontracting, have themselves become outsource providers. These include spectacular examples such as IBM and Digital Equipment.

SCI is a world leader in contract manufacturing. It evolved from a small research company selling into the space craft industry in the 1970s. SCI now produces components, full systems and even provides volume production for customers using a range of electronics from computers and telecoms to automobiles, satellite dishes and consumer systems.

Many of the larger companies have recently entered this business to attempt to leverage under-utilised capacity or to add value to distribution networks. The competitiveness of the traditional suppliers tends to be expressed in cost edge, flexibility and technical capacity. SCI is in the extraordinary situation of seeing some of its biggest customers become its competitors.

Some of the smaller companies believe, and say privately, that large OEMs, such as Digital and IBM, cannot compete with them because of their high cost structures and their lack of contract experience. If such large companies are given business, it is not clear what happens to their interest in this new business should their own core businesses take off again.

And this raises some very large questions. Can any enterprise be a big manufacturer and a big buyer of outsourced suppliers and, at the same time, offer its own services as an outsource supplier? And are not the very desirable attributes on offer from dynamic SME suppliers special only to them? And finally, is not the fact that the large OEMs are desperately downsizing in itself evidence that they are not really in the best position to diversify into such a competitive area?

The OEMs, particularly in Europe, however, have one great advantage. They already have all the necessary certifications and other qualifications needed for the market? These could include ISO 9000, BS 7750, the CE Mark, IEC certification, and product certifications.

Despite some OEMs going into the supply of outsourced services, many OEMs are in fact withdrawing from component manufacture. Many contract manufacturers are very big in their own right, as are many component manufacturers in general engineering industries contrary to the general assumption that outsource suppliers are all small compared with big OEM buyers.

SCI Systems, Inc., for example, with 19 plants worldwide, is a multinational diversified electronics manufacturer whose products and systems are supplied to a variety of aerospace, industrial and commercial customers. SCI has sales of over $1697.1 million. SCI Europe employs over 1500 people in its plants in Ireland and Scotland.

An important trend in contract manufacturing is the growing willingness of customers to allow the contract manufacturer to become involved in field support. This appears to be happening also across the wide spectrum of services now amenable to outsourcing.

The main issues influencing the decision to employ contract manufacturers are, in order of priority: high production costs, high (capital) cost of equipment, scheduling demands (including equipment tooling and set up), demands for flexibility (many caused by shorter lead times), and the need to give greater priority to such core activities as research and development and design.

In looking for an outsourcing partner, OEMs rank the following criteria in this order of priority: quality delivery (zero defect), price, technology capability, delivery capacity (including location) and financial stability. Low on the list are the size of the potential supplier and his in-house R & D capabilities.

Contract manufacturing has been growing in the electronics industry at a rate which has far exceeded that of the electronics industry itself, with Asia leading as a supplier in the market, followed by the US and Europe.

Contract manufacturing is examined in more depth in Chapter 12.

Automotive industry

Probably the biggest element causing an upsurge in outsourcing in the automotive industry is new technology.

New sensors, or 'electronic control units', are emerging at a remarkable rate giving rise to great opportunities for suppliers who believe that they are better placed to manufacture them than is the automotive industry itself, as the new devices may be compatible with what they were already making for the computer industry.

Diversification into, or the exploitation of the outsourcing trend in, this new automotive market is one of the main technical or management reasons for the current expansion of SCI's European manufacturing facilities, aided by diversification into other markets such as telecoms, satellite television, point of sale and medical (see Chapter 14).

Pierre Jocou, who was then the chief executive of the car quality division of the merging Renault–Volvo company, a merger that was later abandoned, confirmed that the company was both outsourcing and 'trimming and very severely reducing suppliers, less and less buying components and more and more buying whole functions. Instead of buying five components and assembling them ourselves, we would ask one supplier to be a leader.'

This is precisely the need that SCI was filling, in the case of the French automotive industry, and it followed their discovery of the potential for diversifying into that industry. This in turn came out of their realisation of the increase in the use of electronic components by European car manufacturers.

Financial houses

Banks and other finance houses are outsourcing. However, the subject is very sensitive to them as many European banks in particular are trying to get rid of long serving and higher paid staff, so little is known about their outsourcing projects. In some high street banks the drop in service levels has been quite notice-able, and competition has increased from building societies. Barclays spotted the outsourcing trend early and formed BCO to supply both their internal needs for mainframe computing (at arm's length from the company and virtually in competition with others) and at the same time to compete with other suppliers such as IBM, Hoskyns and ICL's CFM (Computer ,Facilities Management).

General manufacturing

General manufacturing has been trimming down and making important alliances with suppliers for a number of years, so per-haps there is less to expect here in the future. All manufacturing plants, however, in line with other businesses, can also outsource IT, buildings management, security and other services such as catering, and many are already doing this. The difference with manufacturing is that it is so far advanced in the process that it is more likely to be concentrating on alliances with both suppliers and other partners, and paying great attention to purchasing and the supply chain.

8 Market testing

The UK government's Market Testing Programme

Background to the programme

Market testing has as its origins a UK government White Paper *Competing for Quality* published in 1991. The government's primary intention was to obtain better value for the money it spends, particularly on those services that were available in the marketplace. Their concern was that this value for money was never really tested and therefore government departments were in the position of monopolistic suppliers.

Market testing is the process by which costs of providing a service in-house are compared with the costs of providing the same or better service from the private sector. In the Foreword of the official document on market testing, published by HMSO in 1991, and entitled *The Government's Guide to Market Testing*, the Rt Hon William Waldegrave MP, then Chancellor of the Duchy of Lancaster, had this to say: 'Market testing is helping to improve the quality and the cost effectiveness of many activities in central government. In promoting the extension of market testing and competitive tendering, we are endeavouring to ensure that competition is both free and fair.'

Compulsory Competitive Tendering

The UK government has also laid down a timetable according to which local authorities must put out their services to competitive tendering. This process is known as Compulsory Competitive Tendering (CCT). Under CCT each aspect of local authority services (such as housing, finance, IT) must have a specified amount tested competitively according to a timetable. For example, 80 per cent of IT services provided by a local authority internally must be put out to competitive tender by the end of 1995.

This is not to say that a private tender will succeed. Indeed, in most cases an in-house bid for the services will be made, either in direct competition with external suppliers or in a collaborative venture. CCT is time and cost consuming for an authority and can be very divisive.

Both the authorities and the potential suppliers of services feel, with some justification, that the process is biased in favour of the other. The in-house team do not feel that they have the commercial skills needed and the external supplier, who will have to make a decision on whether to embark on a costly tendering process, could feel that the incumbent supplier has the advantage.

The strategy

The UK government's Market Testing Programme is no less a project than a government reinventing itself. The programme requires civil servants, and those running publicly owned enterprises, to compete against the private sector for work they are currently doing through the processes of testing the market for outsourcing possibilities and putting certain work out for compulsory competitive tender – up to £1.4 billion worth of public services in the period 1993–4. One of these contracts, the largest outsourcing agreement ever in Europe, was to pass £41.5 billion worth of work over ten years from the UK's Inland Revenue to EDS (Electronic Data Systems Corporation) representing the handing over of the tax collection system, plus many of its staff, to private enterprise.

In addition to both market testing and compulsory tendering, a citizen's charter has been drawn up, setting out standards for the operation of the public service. This has been described as 'better public services contributing to a better Britain Incorporated performance', by Brian Hilton, the head of the Citizen's Charter unit. Examples of the results of this charter can be seen in the targets for punctuality and reliability published by British Rail and London Underground.

The padded and complacent bureaucracy which led to this revolution in approach to services was responsible for massive overspending and abysmal service standards in the Department of Social Security, and an almost threefold increase in costs over not many more years in other bodies.

Concentration on core competencies is at the centre of the strategy, together with getting rid of monstrous inefficiencies. Its intention is that central government will focus on policy making, while efficient private sector organisations will deliver services, giving taxpayers a better deal at lower cost.

Interest from other governments

Other governments are watching with interest. The Washington administration is already at work on a similar programme in the US, where three federal agencies, the Internal Revenue Service, the Social Security Administration, and the US Postal Service, all of which have poor service records, have to adopt a citizen's charter concept. Asked if this meant that the US was following Britain, White House official, David Osborne, replied, 'We are following in their footsteps. We took their notion of promising a certain level of service delivery and made deals with agencies here.'

The interest in the process is so great from overseas that Peninah Thomson, a Coopers & Lybrand consultant who advises overseas governments on ministries, sees it as a potential export service, saying, 'Public service reform has become an invisible export for Britain.' Malaysia has been reaping benefits from the approach for at least ten years, having privatised or outsourced almost its entire public service, and it is possible that Malaysia was a benchmark for the UK.

Reaction to the programme

When Group 4 took over part of the prison services and let some prisoners escape, there was rejoicing in the public service unions. But the slip was a small hitch in a process which appears unstoppable, as if that process also is part of a global trend in a world no longer able to tolerate incompetence and waste.

Britain has five million public sector employees, one out of every five workers, so a negative reaction was inevitable. John N. Ellis, secretary of the Council of Civil Service Unions, an umbrella organisation representing 400 000 public workers, understandably attacked the plan, with the message that it would allow 'public corruption on a scale seen only in Italy'. Late in 1993, civil servants staged a one-day strike, which was the largest for more than a decade. Even the Tower of London was closed to tourists.

Operation of the programme

The programme is operating at both national and local levels. The local changes may in the long run be the more revolutionary as they are returning power to the community by encouraging people to 'think local'. Examples range from the outsourcing of the collection of parking fines to managing schools. Some housing agencies now have no houses; instead they have become enabling authorities which decide what to do while others decide how to do it.

The central civil service has been divided into 92 agencies, each headed by a chief executive who is charged with performance targets set by government ministers and whose pay is related to performance. While the best example of market testing so far has been the planned outsourcing of Inland Revenue, a huge array of business is becoming available, from helping the Customs to keep out drug importers to managing hospitals.

The Home Office is putting all its personal computer (PC) procurement out to tender, with contracts on offer worth millions of pounds. According to John Neil at the Home Office procurement department, 'We don't know the full extent of the services we shall need yet, so we are keeping our options open and making it a broad requirement. We may not award contracts for all of it.

If suppliers are able to offer an entire package, then we would be willing to consider it. But bids must be competitive in all areas. I have yet to be convinced that suppliers offering services can be as cost effective as the in-house facility. My concern is with hardware dealers. I would not like to see them recouping reduced margins on services.'

In 1993 the annual expenditure of the UK Civil Service on contracted out activities was £1.5 billion. By the end of 1997 it may reach £10 billion. UK government sources estimate that savings from contracting out can range from 6 per cent to 25 per cent. Local authorities have already contracted out £2 billion worth of services – principally refuse collection, cleaning of buildings, maintenance of grounds, street cleaning, sports and leisure management, vehicle maintenance and catering. The same is happening now with the contracting out of the management of hospitals and health centres. Government will contract out such functions as audit, accountancy, payroll, personnel, and legal. Even sea surveillance for HM Customs and Excise is being contracted out.

TUPE

TUPE – Transfer of Undertakings (Protection of Employment) Regulations 1981 – was the UK government's effort at enshrining the EC Acquired Rights Directive in UK law. It has had a chequered history in the UK, not least because of the uncertainty over its applications to outsourcing contracts.

The original intention of TUPE was to protect entitlement to continued employment under the same terms and conditions in the event of a transfer of the work in which an employee is engaged to another organisation. It applies to salary and to certain benefits but does not extend to providing the same pension benefits as in the previous contract. One early confusion arose over the exclusion of businesses that 'were not in the nature of a commercial venture', which was interpreted to exclude outsourcing of local authority or other government work. This anomaly was corrected in 1993 with the UK's Trade Union Reform and Employment Rights Act 1993, known as TURER.

A recent ruling by the European Court of Justice found the UK to be in breach of the Acquired Rights Directive on several points, including the exclusion of non-profit making organisations and for not providing sufficient financial penalty for any failure to properly inform or consult. In the light of this ruling and recent test cases, it is expected that the UK government will extend TUPE to comply with the Acquired Rights Directive in respect of government and healthcare sector employees.

The application or otherwise of TUPE has largely been based on precedents set by the various court cases over the years. Organisations looking at outsourcing contracts, either from the point of view of the vendor or the client organisation, have usually had to assess whether or not TUPE applies and, where it does, design an outsourcing contract on the assumption that the employees involved enjoy continued employment on the same terms and conditions as before.

There are probably few outsourcing situations to which TUPE will not apply, as most of them, whether in the private or public sector, will be within the spirit of the Acquired Rights Directive, even if not all cases are yet enshrined in UK law. It is therefore recommended that in negotiating outsourcing contracts both parties should assume that TUPE applies, unless there are exceptional circumstances in which case expert legal advice should be sought. The lack of certainty and the problems posed by TUPE have led to a marked downturn in enthusiasm for the Market Testing Programme.

Procord and British Gas took the decision jointly that they would enter into an outsourcing relationship on the assumption that the TUPE legislation applied to the affected employees. They did this largely because the legislation had not been tested by precedent, and because they were more concerned with the proper continuity of service.

British Gas staff involved in the move to Procord were given three options: take redundancy pay; take redundancy and apply to join Procord on new terms; or transfer on existing terms within

British Gas. Equally, they could have been shunted into Procord whether they liked it or not.

According to a spokesman: 'It would have been easy to take a hard line and say everyone had to transfer. That is not good from a people point of view and it is not good from a services point of view because if people are unhappy they do not perform. Staff were introduced to our way of operating so that they could compare us as employers. We gave them the telephone numbers of all our employees so they could ring up anyone they wanted and get the message, warts and all.' Within two days of the contract being signed staff seminars were under way.

The role of the EU

Tendering for supply for most services under either market testing or compulsory tendering are subject to the EU Services Directive (Council Directive 90/50/EEC) from 1 July 1993. This lays down rules for advertising and award of contract. Procedures may be open, restricted, or negotiated. Most UK government services will be acquired under the negotiated procedure.

Acknowledgement is due to both Turner Kenneth Brown, solicitors, and HMSO for helpful material on this subject.

Reference publications on market testing and CCT
Competing for Quality, (1991), London, HMSO, CM1730

Market Testing for IS/IT Provision, (May 1993), London, CCTA, (ISBN: 0946683'645)

PCPU Guidance Note No. 34: *Market Testing and Buying In*, (1992), London, HM Treasury

9 · Information technology

PA survey on IT outsourcing

In 1993 PA Consulting Group, UK conducted a survey of business and information technology directors' experiences and views of IT outsourcing. The key findings from their survey were:

- There is widespread and growing use of outsourcing in all aspects of information technology, from strategy through to delivery.
- This use is chiefly tactical, with short-term contracts covering only a few aspects of an organisation's IT rather than large, long-term, strategic contracts for substantial IT service provision.
- The benefits of outsourcing are not just in cost cutting, but also in the delivery of business and IT service improvements.
- Achieving the benefits is by no means straightforward – most organisations lack the critical skills needed to embark on a new sourcing strategy and to manage their outsourced contracts.
- There are high levels of concern about IT outsourcing, with

105

significant numbers of organisations reporting problems of cost escalation, over-independence and a lack of flexibility from their suppliers.

- IT outsourcing is increasingly popular, but both the purchasers and suppliers must work to establish mutual confidence.
- The proportion considering outsourcing is broadly the same as the proportion who are not considering it.

Some detailed findings and commentary on them follow.

Of those surveyed, 74 per cent were already outsourcing some IT services, or were considering it. This is a big increase from three years previously when the US Yankee Group survey showed that two-thirds were opposed to outsourcing.

Over 70 per cent of contracts were for less than £1 million and 78 per cent were for three years or less. This signals a change from data centre facilities management, where operations could easily account for 30–50 per cent of the IT budget, to more tactical outsourcing. It also shows that large outsourcing projects account for only a small number of contracts.

There is more caution being demonstrated, possibly what is known as 'smartsourcing', or fragmenting the operations into more manageable pieces so that they can be evaluated separately and independently as candidates for outsourcing. For example, it may be beneficial to outsource the help desk part of operations, rather than employ the wide range of skills needed to support all the installed applications and PCs.

IT organisations are moving from internally focused management information systems (MIS) to service-led MIS. This change means that they are focusing on the performance of the services they are delivering to users as opposed to the traditional data centre operations. This again is enabling them to pick off services that are more readily outsourced. For example, the traditional IT department used to measure things like the central processing unit (CPU) utilisation, disk storage, lines of code written and so on. The wise ones today are measuring things like number of outstanding user requests, availability of the computing service, mean time to fix problems and number of applications right first time – all of which are aspects of customer service.

The most frequently outsourced services

The 11 services most actively considered as candidates for outsourcing, according to the survey, were:

1   systems and technical strategy
2   business analysis
3   systems analysis and design
4   application development and implementation
5   network design and implementation
6   data centre operations
7   network operations
8   applications maintenance
9   technical support
10   end-user support
11   help desk.

(The above activities are shown graphically, so the numbers do not correspond to the order of activity.)

1   Systems and technical strategy

Not surprisingly systems and technical strategy was outsourced the least actively. There is little value that a current supplier can provide, so this is usually bought as consultancy. Unless there are good reasons to do otherwise, this will probably be one of the functions to keep in-house. It is also the key linkage between the business and the technology functions or layers of management.

2   Business analysis

Business analysis was the second least actively outsourced service. It is not a function lending itself to outsourcing as it requires continuous management responsibility and close linkages with what is increasingly a changing business climate.

3   Systems analysis and design

Systems analysis and design, once again, was not outsourced frequently.

4   *Application development and implementation*

A growing area of outsourcing is application development and implementation. ICI Agrochemicals was one of the pioneers in this area, transferring 60 development staff to Hoskyns and buying back a development service. On the plus side, it gives access to a wider range of skills and current new technologies such as object orientation and client server. On the minus side, companies may be locked into monopoly supply of software development skills without being able to test value for money. Big development shops such as BT, who currently use a large number of expensive individual contractors, were planning to outsource the management of this function. A service contract with one supplier is easier to manage and control and less expensive than dealing with many contract staff.

5   *Network design and implementation*

Network design and implementation and the operation of networks will be a high growth area. Design and implementation will mostly be bought as consultancy or project work, however, as companies will tend to want it as a discrete or one off rather than a continuous service. A possible exception is local area network cabling. This is often in a permanent state of flux as organisations change and grow.

6   *Data centre operations*

The operation of data centres was the earliest example of the outsourcing of an IT function, referred to as Facilities Management, though this term has now come to refer to the management of buildings and associated services by companies such as Procord. Although still the largest sector of the IT outsourcing market, the survey concludes that the outsourcing of data centres is slowing significantly and this slowdown in market growth is mirrored in other research findings by companies such as Input Corporation.

7   *Network operations*

Multi-vendor, multi-standard, multi-country and multi-applications are some of the complex characteristics of networks today.

The growth of networked applications and the demand for high capacity bandwidth applications, such as video on demand, means that companies will have to rely on the specialist network management companies for management of this operation. Unlike data centre operations, this is about more than cost cutting, even though the outsource supplier can perhaps negotiate a better tariff with the national telecom companies – post, telegraph and telecommunications organisations (PTTs).

Examples of this service being outsourced are Digital operating Quotron's network worldwide, and BT's Syncordia managing Glaxo's private network across the US, UK and Canada.

8 Applications maintenance

Applications maintenance is still the most frequently outsourced function, just ahead of applications development and technical support. The old legacy systems containing the billions of lines of Cobol code, written in the 1970s and 1980s, will not go away just because someone has invented client server and object orientation. These applications are still the backbone of most commercial computing and need to be nurtured. Maintenance has been a distraction to many IT organisations trying to meet the demands of their companies for new systems.

9 Technical support

Another popular function for outsourcing is technical support. One reason for this is that the single vendor, single architecture approach has been replaced by a more complex technical world. Despite open systems it is now the IT organisation which has to be the integrator, maintainer and supporter of these new information technology systems, which are independent of any one major equipment supplier, a state known as 'vendor independent'.

10/11 End user support and help desk

The outsourcing of both end user support and help desk is also driven by the complexity of the technology. Few organisations are large enough to justify keeping all the skills in-house which are necessary to support the range of bought-in PC hardware, local area networks and applications which now proliferate in many organisations. At the same time, PC re-sellers have found this a high value added source of revenue. The days when the re-seller sold PC hardware and walked away are gone. When a PC is sold today the purchaser will be offered everything from integration of software, siting and cabling, and user training to help desk support and maintenance.

IT managers no longer feel threatened

'Turkeys do not vote for Christmas' was a criticism levelled at certain IT managers who resisted looking at the benefits of outsourcing for fear it might cost them their job. The survey found this not to be true, but that on the contrary IT directors led the way in outsourcing and staff were prepared to look outside to get the best service for their companies.

Difference between public and private sectors

In the public sector, PA had expected the level of activity to be spurred on by market testing, or the obligation to compare value for money from internal service provision with that from the private sector (see Chapter 8). IT services have been obvious candidates for early testing, but despite this there is little difference between the outsourcing activities of the public and private sectors. The public sector is marginally more likely to outsource services such as systems and technical strategy and business analysis, but there is no clear cut distinction.

Benefits of outsourcing

Cost savings is the most popular expected benefit (55 per cent), but around 30 per cent reported no savings, while one quarter of those who expected cost savings were disappointed. Better access to specialist IT skills was reported as the key benefit achieved.

The clear message is that outsourcing is not just about cost cutting; it can deliver business and IT service improvements as well.

For example, 44 per cent of the IT directors and 33 per cent of business directors see head count reductions as a desirable outcome from outsourcing. Over 42 per cent of business directors are expecting better access to improved technology, compared with some 24 per cent of IT directors. This could reflect the continuing concern of some business directors that in-house IT organisations cannot keep pace with technology development.

Problems with suppliers

There were a large number of concerns and problems relating to the service provided by the supplier. The most frequently reported are listed below in order of magnitude:

1   overdependence
2   cost escalation
3   lack of flexibility
4   maintaining quality
5   lack of supporting management skills.

The wide range and high number of problems which have been experienced with suppliers may have arisen as a result of supplier dominated negotiations and contracts. As the survey puts it: 'suppliers do it every day – clients only infrequently', so the suppliers have the experience.

Skills shortage

The skills needed to manage the supplier relationship were frequently underestimated. More organisations experienced problems in this area than had expected to do so, especially in the public sector where the figure reached 67 per cent.

A significant number of respondents reported a shortage of key skills required to outsource IT successfully. There is broad agreement both in the public and private sectors and in large and small IT organisations about the need for new skills to negotiate, implement and manage IT outsourcing arrangements.

IT and business directors differed in their assessment of skills shortages. For the typical business director, the greatest need is for skills early in the process to define a sourcing strategy and analyse the market for IT services. In contrast, by far the biggest concerns for IT directors are preparing service level agreements and managing suppliers after the award of contracts.

Conclusions of the survey

For some organisations, the buying-in of IT services is regarded as a valuable tool in:

- gaining access to certain new skills
- smoothing peaks and troughs of demand
- providing a means of demonstrating the value for money being delivered in-house.

For others, it is much more a question of securing the longer-term supply of up-to-the minute technology and IT skills and the rapid delivery of new applications, backed up by the formality and rigour of service legal agreements.

Professional and expert advice, independent of service suppliers and internal parties, has an important part to play in delivering the full benefits from outsourcing. Experience, skill and objectivity are essential in identifying realistic objectives, adopting the correct IT outsourcing strategy, and ensuring successful contract negotiations and management. With the right skills early in the decision process, more businesses could achieve the desired results and avoid the pitfalls.

If you want to assess what IT outsourcing offers your organisation you should:

- separate your internal advisory and delivery roles
- develop or acquire the skills needed to define and implement a sourcing strategy
- determine your sourcing strategy and implementation plan
- implement.

Above all, you need to be properly prepared before discussing opportunities and possible responses with potential suppliers.

'The Yankee 100' survey

The US research company, The Yankee Group, carried out a survey of over 100 companies most of whom, but not all, are US based. The findings were published in 1993 in a report entitled 'The Yankee 100'.

The purpose of outsourcing

In order of importance the purpose of outsourcing by the companies surveyed was:

- to control IT costs
- to accomplish change
- to gain expertise
- to improve IT generally
- to make IT more responsive
- to off-load management
- to focus on core business
- to liquidate (get rid of function).

While the third most common reason for outsourcing was the gaining of expertise, success in achieving this was the number one result achieved.

Company satisfaction

The study asked companies if they were satisfied with the following requirements and processes:

- understanding business needs
- transition management
- communication/reporting
- change management process
- problem management process
- technical capability
- cost and fees
- service level attainment
- response to changes in needs.

Expectations were met, although not often exceeded, on all these points except for transition management.

Benefits sought from outsourcing

The Yankee Group used the heading *The Importance of Being Expert* to observe: 'The cases reinforce the point the Yankee 100 has already stated – that expertise is an important value sought in outsourcing.

'In traditional outsourcing arrangements the "expertise" was in the area of efficient operation of a data centre running batch and on-line transaction processing (OLTP) applications. Today, there is much more variety and complexity at both the system level (from mainframes to networks, desktop, and client/server) and the applications level (from batch and OLTP application to office, work flow, decision support, and more). This increases the complexity and expense needed to master IT, and increases opportunities to make wise use of the outsourcing approach.'

In addition to cost containment, the benefits sought from outsourcing by 107 respondents are shown below (in order of importance):

Benefits sought	Percentage of companies
expertise	36
quality/improvement/excellence	25
timeliness (better lead times)	18
reliability, stability	13
track record (to improve image)	10
improved business	9
temporary (where an opportunity to concentrate on other things was obtained)	8
cost	8
fit	7
new technology	6
transfer (the report is not clear about what this particular benefit is, but probably move the function within the company)	3
none	3

Companies opposed to outsourcing

The following table shows the percentage of companies opposed to outsourcing:

Year	*Companies opposed to outsourcing*
1989	66%
1990	51%
1991*	34.5%

* This figure shows how rapidly outsourcing came to be an accepted strategy in the IT managers' armoury; from outright resistance in 1989 to a complete reversal in 1991. Yankee Group ceased asking this question at this time. Today they believe that there is no organisation that would oppose outsourcing as a strategy.

Projected growth

The percentage of Yankee 100 respondents who were signing outsourcing contracts had risen from 2 per cent in 1989 to 19 per cent in 1993. Total expenditures on outsourcing worldwide of these companies rose from $26 billion in 1989 to $50 billion in 1994.

Partnerships

Virtual

- Customer's data centre is used as a base for added business growth from other customers to the vendor.
- All revenues go to the vendor.
- Savings/revenues realised by the vendor keep customer costs down.
- Vendor usually assumes all staff, equipment, and occupancy expenses.

Real

- Vendor and customer form a legal partnership – a new company.

- Expenses are shared jointly.
- Revenues are shared jointly.
- Vendor is likely to supply all sales and marketing support.
- May include issues of confidentiality, where perhaps confidentiality issues are so critical that only this form will suffice.

The value-added business function

In cases where there is real benefit in terms of value added to the process, the following were seen to be involved:

- The vendor must have significant line-of-business knowledge.
- There is less need for the vendor to be the low-cost bidder.
- The vendor may be well established in certain vertical markets.
- Before the value added is achieved, it may quantify and sell.

Risk-benefit sharing

Expected savings or increased revenues not realised could have a financial impact for both the vendor and customer:

- Added business from new customers may never be realised.
- There may be unexpected increases in operational expense to support new customers.
- The vendor may implement a new system giving rise to increased business with a share in the resulting increased profit going to the vendor.
- The vendor could re-design work flow and cause disruption and extra training costs.

The authors are indebted to Susan McGarry, Vice President, The Yankee Group, for the above information.

The development of IT outsourcing

While IT has not been associated with outsourcing for as long as say catering and security, companies first employed outside facilities management providers of IT back in the 1960s. The original driver was confusion over, and fear of, computers, which were a black art performed by people who did not always fit into the company culture. These people, for example, did not always justify what they did and may have been seen to be demanding more money to do it.

EDS, the most successful outsourcer of the time, changed this by offering to control costs, explain what they were doing in their language and take away the mystique. They were also prepared to make their people conform and wear suits and ties.

EDS fitted the corporate style of the time, and so they were believed and welcomed with open arms. They did not even have to promise to do things at a lower cost. They had little competition, apart from the in-house staff that they were about to take over, and so could charge premium prices for the service.

The profit margins open to EDS, and to the other early players, were huge. One EDS veteran is quoted as saying, 'In the early 1980s, I could guarantee without even setting foot inside the door of a data centre that I could save 20 per cent of their budget and provide a better service than they were getting in-house.'

The infrastructure issues of the 1970s and early 1980s were huge. Profits could be made simply on the basis of reducing the power consumption of a mainframe computer complex. In the 1990s, however, their are few places where there is room for similar savings in the cost of computer operations. This is why there is a falling off in the traditional facilities management market. Many economies have been obtained, either in-house or through the use of outsourcing.

There are, however, economies of scale in other areas, for example application maintenance. Companies like the FI Group are taking on programming departments with as many as 100 people at a time, such as Whitbread in the UK, along with contracts to maintain the 'legacy' applications, usually mainframe-based and written in Cobol. Like EDS in the 1970s, they have little competition, are making good profits and are giving a quality service. The sales pitch of 'This is how you can get rid of the millstone of maintenance and free your people to develop the new applications that are needed to grow your business' has attractions for companies faced with maintaining millions of lines of

Cobol 'code', a backlog of new applications and a general skills shortage in the market.

IT has spearheaded much of the progress in outsourcing over the past 30 years. It broke a commercial mould of vertical integration with in-house advertising departments, cleaning services and catering. Henry Ford wanted pig iron to go in at one end and model Ts to roll out the other, with Ford workers doing everything that was needed in between.

Complexity and competition changed all of that as new industrial practices took over and outside specialists emerged who could do certain work more efficiently.

The current state of IT outsourcing

IT vendor companies such as Digital and IBM, together with research organisations, such as Input, Yankee, and others, all concur that outsourcing is the fastest growing sector in the IT market, growing at 20–30 per cent a year. As IT is a mature function, this is an indication of the general growth of outsourcing and of the great potential for other functions. Digital believes that 400 of the top 500 organisations are or will outsource at least one IT function by 1996.

Companies are outsourcing to reduce operational costs, to increase speed of response – that is reduce cycle times – and also to achieve value enhancement both to existing business and through innovation.

They are improving the balance sheet by removing fixed assets (equipment supported activities), staying in tune with rapidly changing technology, securing access to scarce skills and achieving guaranteed service levels.

Many of the large computer or IT companies are also offering outsourcing services. IBM, for example, is wanting to both give work to outsource suppliers and be an outsource supplier itself.

Hewlett-Packard has also set up a division dedicated to outsourcing. In its UK support centre alone it generated £100 million in revenues through the supply of outsourcing and related services in its first year. Its original plan was not to compete directly with outsourcing giants such as EDS and Computer Sciences but to stay within its own customer base, offering a restricted range of outsourcing services which did not include the taking over of entire data centres. In their words, 'Outsourcing has grown into a very diverse market and selective outsourcing is a definite trend in the market place.'

In its own sales campaign to obtain outsourcing business, Digital quotes the prescription by US management guru Tom Peters to 'do what you do best and outsource the rest'. It believes that 'traditional' facilities management with its emphasis on out-sourcing data centre, or mainframe-based networks and systems is fast becoming commoditised (the expression used by computer people to describe when a product becomes a commodity as distinct from one related to a manufacturer, such as IBM or Micro-soft), that entry costs are low and new outsource providers are encouraged to enter the market by current annual growth of between 20 per cent and 30 per cent.

Digital and others believe that outsourcing is increasingly driven by recessionary pressures to re-engineer the company balance sheets in which fixed costs are prefaced by variable costs. In a business environment that achieves dramatically improved business performance rather than merely reducing IT costs, the most successful suppliers are those which best understand their customers' business and can add value to that business.

Current facilities management growth rates of 20–30 per cent in the UK are also being sustained by the desire of corporations to access specialist, value-added skills which either they do not have internally or are proving cost-prohibitive to maintain as the move back to focusing strictly on core business gathers momentum.

So many companies are outsourcing the IT function that only the spectacular examples appear in the media, the Inland Revenue and British Aerospace being the most quoted. The Woolwich Building Society awarded a £3 million application management contract to IMI Computing. Explaining why this company was given the business rather than larger competitors, David Benaron, head of computer development at the Woolwich, explained: 'The decision was very close. But we chose IMI Computing because we felt it would fit in more appropriately with our culture. We were impressed by its other reference sites, such as Legal & General and the fact that it could deliver on time.'

10 Outsourcing the business process

While information technology has become established as an outsourced service worldwide, it is also one of the many components of the business process or function which are now being outsourced. This is being called 'business operations outsourcing', in the US, while in the UK it is also known as 'managed services'.

We are indebted to Input for much of the information in this section.

Reasons for outsourcing business operations

Most organisations in Europe are already undertaking or considering the kinds of business re-engineering which may lead to outsourcing, much of which results in the outsourcing of IT, and this is leading to the wider practice of business operations outsourcing. This can involve entire business functions or processes, and its purpose is to allow increased operational flexibility and better focus on core activities.

According to a report by Input, *Business Operations Outsourcing, Europe* published in 1994, the main advantage of this is that the supplier is able to optimise effectiveness when it is responsible for the whole process. The concept of outsourcing business operations may have been helped by suppliers moving from running computer operations to the 'systems integration' of all IT, whereby suppliers take over the development and running of all IT related business.

Characteristics of the market

The beginnings of the latest trend in business operations outsourcing in Europe were signalled by the contract between BP Exploration and Andersen Consulting in 1991. By 1993, Input identified an existing market of $150 million. One third of this was within the public sector in the UK, where the expression 'managed services' began to be heard. The activity is posing a threat to those vendors who offer to outsource IT only which is most interesting as it mirrors a process already well under way in industry worldwide – that of customers seeking to purchase more and more from single suppliers.

Input established the following characteristics of the market:

● Administrative functions were prime candidates for business operations outsourcing.
● The process of outsourcing the business operations was an alternative to moving from the outsourcing of IT elements to the systems integration of IT.

Perhaps the most dramatic conclusion of the report was that business operations outsourcing would grow more rapidly than the information systems outsourcing market over the years to 1999, although the existing IT outsourcing market is of course much more mature than others.

Examples of the kinds of business process which Input examined are books and magazine administration for Time Life, parking fines collection in Seville, Spain, the accounting function for BP Exploration and the administration of BP's share register dealings. Although there were millions of transactions annually in the Time Life job, it seems that transaction volume is not in itself a significant factor in the decision to outsource a business process.

The driving forces behind the decisions to outsource business functions were:

- core business focus
- need for cost savings
- as a result of benchmarking
- a re-engineering exercise.

What also emerged from the BP Exploration–Andersen Consulting agreement, was that clients may find it preferable to let a vendor take over a whole process and re-engineer it as necessary rather than attempt to re-engineer it themselves.

The Input study found that companies are more likely to outsource labour intensive operations, particularly where they show considerable peaks and troughs of activity, and operations which they perceive to be commonplace and not unique to their own organisations.

Outsourcing core activities

The Input study also helps to expose the myth that organisations will not outsource activities that are a part of their core business and provide them with competitive advantage, as companies are already doing just this. The study pointed to Vauxhall outsourcing its Customer Assistance Centre to EDS, which gave rise to what was described as 'a substantial rise in customer satisfaction as well as an increase in those prepared to recommend Vauxhall products'.

The study suggests that there are few core activities which cannot be outsourced at the administrative and operational levels. There is, however, an important proviso, which reads *provided that the client retains the means of establishing policy and direction, together with the means to monitor service delivery and manage the vendor.*

In other words, the owner company must retain the means of establishing policy, which in relevant circumstances means maintaining or changing policy which has already been established. Direction has to mean strategy, as distinct from day-to-day tactics, and plans if any to make changes. Retaining the means to monitor service delivery is vital as companies will not want to be in ignorance about customer service levels. Measurements under the ISO 9000 quality management system will be useful here. Finally, the principal must be able to manage the vendor, so avoiding a situation in which the vendor begins to operate as a law unto themselves, and even believes that they 'own' the service.

Re-engineering by the vendor

According to the Input study, the propensity to outsource high cost–labour intensive business processes implies that business operations outsourcing involves transferring responsibility for re-engineering a business process from the client to the vendor. This assumes that a business process is outsourced before the client tries to re-engineer it so the vendor can carry out the re-engineering with a fresh approach, whereas outsource decisions usually follow at least an attempt to re-engineer a process by the client. The report cites examples of re-engineering and systems integration taking place after transfer to the vendor in cases of parking fine administration and insurance claims administration.

The report summed up the three different approaches which vendors might take when offering to take over the business process:

1   re-engineer and expand an existing service such as IT
2   take on the business process with a view to its subsequent re-engineering
3   extend an existing processing service to the wider business process operation.

An example of the third is CMG (Computer Management Group)

Ltd, which has traditionally offered bureau services for payroll and share registration and is now offering to extend these to the full business process. It has extended its payroll service by offering to handle both employee enquiries and liaise with the tax authorities.

Developments in the market

The Input report found that the IT vendors with the greatest ability to offer business operations were EDS and GSI in France, but that this ability was at a low level generally amongst IT vendors. While this could be a serious weakness for equipment and many services vendors, it is expected to change as the business operations market matures. The leading UK vendors in business operations outsourcing were seen to be Capita Group and CSC.

In the general commercial sector, the report found that EDS and Andersen Consulting were the market leaders. Andersen has four major business operations outsourcing contracts, including the accounting functions of three oil companies. EDS has two major European parking fine administration systems and fulfilment services for Time Life.

The Input study expects the business operations market to grow at 27 per cent per annum from 1993 to 1998 to a size of $500 million. The major source of growth in the UK over the next five years will be local government. This is fuelled by the fact that councils must introduce compulsory competitive tendering by October 1996 for finance, corporate administration and personnel, which account for 65 per cent of their activities. Other functions that must also be offered to tender include housing administration and legal services (see Chapter 8).

Input Corporation has offices all over the world. It can be reached in the UK at Piccadilly House, 33/37 Regent Street, London, SW1Y 4NF (telephone: (0171) 493 9335). The *Business Operations Outsourcing, Europe* report quoted is just one of several available from Input on all aspects of IT outsourcing.

11 Building and property management

A summer 1994 supplement in *The Times* on the suppliers of facilities management in the areas of buildings and related services described a thriving business in the supply of contract services in these areas. It also revealed that many companies, which were formerly in the construction business, were now providing a range of support services – a build it and manage it portfolio.

Range of services

Amongst the advertisers, Matthew Hall listed the following range of services: facilities management, estate and grounds, mechanical and electrical maintenance, messenger and mail, reception, cleaning, portering, security, energy management, transport, fabrics and civil, and support services/administration.

The range is huge. Maintenance, including mechanical and electrical, energy management and fabrics, all go well together. Indeed, any builder would now appear to be missing opportunities by not offering such services to the owners of the buildings he has constructed.

Energy management is one of the key environmental issues which have come under the scrutiny of management, together with the other traditional environmental issues – public safety, staff health and safety, and materials conservation. The ideal energy manager is the buildings facilities contractor, especially if that person also designed or supplied the energy and related insulation and control systems in the first instance.

New regulations

There are, at the moment, a number of pressing new regulatory demands on management which are coming from the following sources: environmental legislation, staff health and safety regulations, public safety (in the case of certain buildings and in particular process plants, both with critical processes and security needs) and product safety. Product safety and much of public safety must remain firmly under the control of process management, but issues relating to environmental legislation and staff health and safety regulations will either be decided by lay-out and operation of building systems, or could be amenable to facilities management.

Construction and lay-out of buildings

Under the 1993 EC Health and Safety Regulations, for example, reflected in each EU member state by local statutory instruments, there is a safe workplace regulation which covers: ventilation, temperature, lighting, workstations, floors, walls, glazing, traffic routes, escalators and travolators, doors and gates, sanitary conveniences, electricity, fire safety and controls systems (such as air conditioning).

Safe equipment

The regulation dealing with safe equipment covers such issues as system stability, guards and protective devices, lighting, temperature, warning systems and maintenance. The VDT regulation takes account not just of the hardware and software, but of both the environment in which the VDU operator is working, and the ergonomics of the workstation, including desk and chair. The European Commission uses VDT in the sense of video display terminal for what the rest of us describe as a VDU or video display unit.

Manual handling

The manual handling regulation addresses such issues as the reasonableness of each load for workers lifting it, the lifting action itself, the spaces in which lifters are working (for example, asking if they have to stoop or step over things) and the strength and height of the lifters.

Other health and safety regulations

Further regulations deal with safety signs, personal protective equipment, pregnant and breast-feeding workers (who need special facilities), young persons at work, work at temporary or mobile sites and so on.

Environmental regulations

The traditional environmental regulations also provide opportunities for contract facilities suppliers. Statutory instruments cover areas such as landscaping, amenities, wildlife, urban renewal, derelict buildings, emissions, discharges, noise (such as the noise from building equipment, compressors and lawnmowers) normal waste and toxic waste.

Implications for supplier and client

These wide-ranging regulations have implications for both the discerning contract facilities management provider and the worried manager who needs assurance that the legalities of the environmental and health and safety regulations are being met. If someone is already supplying the full range of buildings facilities management services, why not also add the management of the environmental and health and safety issues, thus opening up a huge new compliance-driven market for building facilities management suppliers? All that is needed is the methodology and that can certainly be developed. While none of the builders offering outsourcing services mentioned these legal-related services, they were on the list of available services from the catering company, Merchant Gardner (see Chapter 13).

The market

The buildings and related market is seen by some to be worth £17 billion per annum, while the University of Strathclyde's Centre for Facilities Management has been quoted as saying that the potential in the UK alone for a wider range of services, such as catering and telecommunications, is around £64 billion.

One of the biggest privatisations in the buildings sector came when the UK government's Property Services Agency at Whitehall was hived off into five separate bodies. The Building and Property Group, which was formed as a result, recruited Matthew Hall's managing director, Clive Groom, as its new chief executive of management services. The company has a turn-over of around £450 million and employs around 3500 people. It has, however, taken over so much government business that the Market Testing Programme itself will now expose it to possible losses of business, as it in turn outsources.

As part of the £10 billion worth of contracted-out expenditure expected from the UK Civil Service by the end of 1997, there will be many buildings related services. Local authorities have already contracted out £2 billion, principally refuse collection, cleaning of buildings, maintenance of grounds, street cleaning, sports and leisure management, vehicle maintenance and catering. This is also happening now with schools, hospitals and health centres (see Chapter 8).

Apart from Matthew Hall, other big construction companies in the business are John Laing, Taylor Woodrow and Mowlem. Mowlem, like IBM and Digital in the IT sector, is both a supplier of outsourced services and an outsource supplier of its own operations.

John Mowlem & Co. has a turnover of £1.5 billion in construction related businesses, and 70 per cent of this is accounted for by purchased materials and subcontracting. Procurement is therefore regarded as a core business and is carried out site by site using small, dedicated teams on a project basis. Like the world class manufacturers, Mowlem looks for, and beyond, JIT and adherence to delivery schedules and price to partnership and, in true outsourcing manner, to those prepared to contribute 'a creative input' to the alliance. Mowlem puts a premium on accurate and timely information and expects the same from its suppliers. The company believes that it has increased its share of the market from 20 per cent to 80 per cent.

Some companies, particularly large original equipment manufacturers (OEMs), find it difficult to both outsource their own activities and offer outsourced services to others. The electronics contract manufacturers believe that neither Digital nor IBM are finding it as easy to offer contract manufacturing as some of their more dedicated rivals such as SCI. However, builders, like publishers, are by nature outsource suppliers, having probably invented 'the lump', the expression used in the trade to describe the employment of the part-timer, the freelancer and the subcontractor, and many of them are now transforming 'the lump' approach into a sophisticated business.

Some, like Laing, are developing the process by acquiring existing management consultancy companies, such as FMS in Yorkshire, and forming an alliance with Andersen Consulting. This second partnership hopes to develop a model which directs a company in its decision whether to use an in-house team or contract out.

There was such management trouble in a large school near Dublin recently – which resulted in management committee squabbles, parent and pupil dissension, and stand offs – that a retired managing director of the national electrical utility was taken on to sort out the problems. Suddenly the school found itself in the new world where, in addition to teaching, teachers must manage efficiently to survive.

The mentality created by the cushion of the safe state job is no preparation for the world of market testing and compulsory competitive tendering. Heads of colleges who thought they were teachers only are now awakening to the fact that they are managers. Nowhere is the case stronger for outsourcing the non-core activities, except perhaps in hospitals.

These non-core activities can range from the project management of new buildings and extensions, already notorious for their tendencies to cost overrun, to catering, cleaning, gymnasium and sport operations, security and maintenance. Catering is such a frequently outsourced service, and has been for so long, that it may be a benchmark against which to assess future developments (see Chapter 13).

12 Contract manufacturing

This chapter summarises a 1993 update of the 1991 report 'Contract Manufacturing from a Global Perspective' prepared by Technology Forecasters, Inc. and is the most comprehensive industry study of the electronic-equipment contract manufacturing market. The 1993 update was sponsored by 14 leading contract manufacturers and electronic equipment companies who focused the topics and questions of the study on to the issues which were most pertinent to this market.

The objective of 'Contract Manufacturing from a Global Perspective' is to generate worldwide estimates, forecasts and trends through reconciling primary and secondary research on contractors, users of contractors and electrical equipment companies that manufacture products in-house. It analyses both contract manufacturers and their customers worldwide in a comprehensive study of the industry and its developments.

The findings in the report are based on detailed interviews with 156 contractors and electronic equipment companies which subcontract manufacturing and conduct manufacturing in-house.

Market summary

Contract manufacturing of electronic equipment

Most of the market estimates and forecasts in the study relate to demand (rather than supply) data-money paid to electronics contract manufacturers by electronic equipment companies for printed circuit board (PCB) assembly and related services. This means that the market figures include the cost of materials for turnkey assembly contracts (in which the contractor purchases the materials on behalf of customers) but do not include the cost of materials for consignment contracts (in which customers provide contractors with kits of materials).

Worldwide demand for electronics contract manufacturing is growing at an average annual rate (AAGR) of approximately 15 per cent from 1992 to 1997. In 1992 the worldwide market for contract manufacturing was about $19.5 billion; by 1997 this market should grow to more than $39 billion. Demand for the worldwide electronic contract manufacturing market for 1992 and 1997 by geographic region is represented in Figure 12.1.

In its 1991 report, *Contract Manufacturing from a Global Perspective*, Technology Forecasters estimated the size of the contract manufacturing industry to be approximately $14.6 billion in 1990, the base year for the report. At $19.5 billion in 1992, the industry had grown at an AAGR of 15.4 per cent during the two years. Growth in contract manufacturing in Asia in the two years was due primarily to growth in the electronics industry. In Europe electronic equipment companies have turned increasingly to contract manufacturers to cut costs and build final systems (which greatly contributes to demand value) in an effort to survive the sluggish economy up to 1994. In Japan and North America contract manufacturing has increased as a popular 'outsourcing' strategy because of the cost-cutting benefits it offers.

Contract manufacturing is growing almost 9 per cent per year faster than electronic equipment production as a whole. This forecast is driven primarily by the electronic equipment companies' increased use of contractors based on complex make-up strategies, including cost cutting strategies. The trend to use contractors

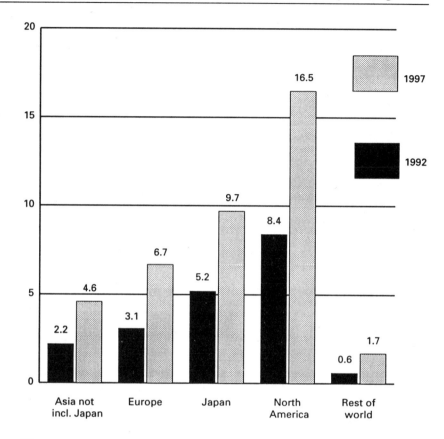

Figure 12.1 Worldwide contract manufacturing demand by region in billions of US dollars, 1992 and 1997
(Source: Technology Forecasters, Inc., Berkeley, California)

for cost cutting and avoidance of capital expenditure is even more prevalent in a downturned economy. Therefore, when overall economic growth forecasts were at the lowest point in 1994 and 1995, the growth in demand for contract manufacturing was at its highest.

In-house PCB costs versus contract manufacturing demand
This section compares in-house and subcontracted PCB assembly and related costs, both globally and regionally. To compare these

costs, in-house costs must be defined to approximate the cost of using contract manufacturers: the in-house PCB assembly costs considered are materials, comprising electronic components, bare PCBs and related supplies, and labour and overhead, comprising manufacturing workers and managers, engineers (including test engineers), purchasing personnel and controls, and depreciation of manufacturing plants and assembly equipment.

The top section of each bar in Figure 12.2 represents in-house PCB assembly and related costs, the bottom represents contract manufacturing demand. Altogether, each full bar represents total cost for PCB assembly and related costs for the years 1992 to 1997. In 1997 the contract manufacturing portion equals 30 per cent of the PCB and related costs.

Technology summary: demand for assembly technologies by contractors' customers

During this forecast period, demand for contract manufacturing of surface mount technology (SMT) PCBs will grow from 61 per cent of total contract manufacturing demand in 1992 to 73 per cent of total demand in 1997.

On average, assembly technologies used in 1992 are similar whether performed in-house or contracted out. Advanced technologies, including chip-on-board (COB), ball grid arrays (BGA) and boards conforming to standards of the Personal Computer Memory Card International Association (PCMCIA), are used to a greater degree in-house than by contractors. However, customers delegate to contractors more fine-pitch, flex-circuit boards, and cable assembly than they perform in-house.

Electronic equipment companies' requirements

The electronic equipment companies interviewed
The 83 electronic equipment manufacturers interviewed represent a broad range of company sizes. Respondents' revenues

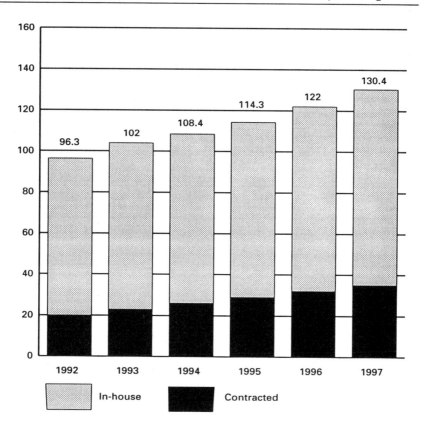

Figure 12.2 In-house PCB assembly and related costs versus demand for contract manufacturing in billions of US dollars, 1992 to 1997
(Source: Technology Forecasters, Inc., Berkeley, California)

for electronic equipment range from less than $1 million to $30 billion. Respondents represent the following regions: North America, Europe, Japan, Asia.

In-house versus subcontracted ratios
Of the companies interviewed, 27 per cent assemble all boards and product units in-house, 17 per cent contract out all electronic equipment assembly, and the remaining 56 per cent assemble boards and electronic equipment both in-house and through contractors to varying degrees.

Of the regions surveyed, North American companies contracted out the largest percentage of their manufacturing in 1992 (56 per cent). Asian companies contracted the smallest percentage of their manufacturing in 1992 (22 per cent) and they plan to slightly increase the percentage contracted to 24 per cent by 1997. European companies plan the largest percentage increase in the amount contracted during the five-year period, from 33 per cent in 1992 to 39 per cent in 1997, primarily as a means of reducing manufacturing costs. Japanese companies, however, show a preference towards returning manufacturing in-house, for reasons of costs, control and proprietary designs.

The study showed an increase in the use of contractors for building complete electronic systems. In 1992 19 per cent of responding companies' payments to contractors was for final system build and this percentage is expected to increase to 23 per cent by 1997.

Trends among contract manufacturers

The 73 contract manufacturers interviewed came from companies of different sizes. Respondents' revenues range from less than $1 million to more than $1 billion.

Contractors' services
Respondents reported that an increasingly large number of contractors are offering services such as final system build, availability to end-users for finished-product services and upgrades, x-ray (or comparable) inspection and documentation reproduction.

Contractors' profitability ratios
The average 1992 net income, as a percentage of overall revenues, for the contractors (worldwide) was 5.1 per cent for 1992. Average return on assets was 24 per cent.

Contractors' productivity ratios and operational data

Operational data	Worldwide respondents' averages
Total number of employees	892
Total square feet	349 000
Percentage of square footage for contract manufacturing	69%
Square feet per employee	282
Inventory turns	8
Sales per square foot	$870
Sales per employee	$103 000

Further information on this and other studies can be obtained from Technology Forecasters, Inc. at 1936 University Ave, Suite 360, Berkeley, California, USA, 94704–1024 (fax 510 849 1997).

13 Catering

According to Clement Freud, there is a school of thought that believes it is not worth putting yourself out for a captive audience. He found this to be true of a river-bank hotel on the Amazon river, where the food was 'exactly as bad as you would expect when the nearest alternative source of nourishment is a four hour chug against the current' and not true of the catering on the Alwyn North platform in the North Sea, where 'meal times assume a rare importance', and where Gardner Merchant provides the catering.

Gardner Merchant Ltd

Gardner Merchant provides an excellent example of those developments in outsourcing known as facilities management. According to the managing director, Garry Hawkes, the contract catering services business has come of age, and is no longer a token reflection of labour relations. In his last company annual report, he explains this as follows: 'Over recent years it has graduated to being a professional service in its own right, in a marketplace where positive, far sighted attitudes can now prevail. Employees who use catering services, patients and schoolchildren are, at last, being seen as customers deserving of quality and choice.'

History

The roots of the present Gardner Merchant organisation go back over 100 years to the late 19th century when John Gardner established his butcher's shop in London's Leadenhall Market. Herbert Merchant did not start out until 40 years later, but, in the process of building that business, he acquired a number of ventures that eventually led along a parallel course to John Gardner and his successors.

From its modest beginning, Gardner's butchery business expanded into provision and supplies. He soon found himself drawn into catering, supplying meals as well as provisions to companies. Herbert Merchant similarly expanded his cigar business into catering after 1929.

During the 1930s Gardner's expansion continued and the firm moved into industrial catering as the rapidly growing motor industry led the way in providing its employees with meals at work. By the end of the war, Merchants had 900 catering contracts, while Gardners were running over 600 canteens and serving 75 000 meals per day.

In 1961 Merchants was acquired by Trust Houses Ltd, as was Gardner three years later, and in 1970 Trust Houses Ltd merged with Forte. Now, with a total of 1600 contracts, the combined Gardner and Merchant business was the largest industrial catering group in the UK.

Many employees must have regretted both merger and takeover when in 1979 Gardner Merchant was losing more contracts than it was winning. The company embarked on a major restructuring programme, strengthened its staff training activities and implemented an ambitious programme of strategic marketing. By 1985 it was gaining three contracts for every one it lost, while in the same period turnover doubled.

In the early 1980s the company acquired Kelvin Catering Company, a leading specialist in site services to the offshore oil industry, and throughout the 1980s and into the 1990s, the company expanded its international operations.

1991 saw the formation of an industry-leading Environmental Services department. This operation includes experienced inspectors all formerly employed by local authorities, as well as the influential health and safety department and a specialist microbiological laboratory. This department enables Gardner Merchant to offer services related to new health and safety regulations (see page 128). It welcomed the 1991 Food Act and initiated company-wide training programmes, the inspection of all sites and the insistence that the regulations were understood and implemented at all levels.

A Commercial Services Division was established to provide facilities management, site services and specialist catering services. The company has now built up the largest and most stable client base in the industry, producing an annual turnover of over £680 million.

In the last five years Gardner Merchant has achieved a world-wide sales increase of more than 250 per cent through steady year on year growth and has produced a 17 per cent compound growth in profits every year since 1987. It has concentrated its operations on the three dynamic regions of Europe, North America and the Far East, where the importance of staff welfare is widely appreciated, and where Gardner Merchant can build its business interests over the long term.

Business outside the UK accounts for 36 per cent of turnover and over 50 per cent of annual growth. Across its three regions, Gardner Merchant has over 44 000 employees, of whom 38 000 are based in Europe, 3800 in North America and over 2300 in the Far East. Operations in Europe, including the UK and Ireland, account for 87 per cent of the company's turnover and a major part of its profit. Continental Europe represents 24 per cent of turnover and employs 8150 people. Over 30 000 people are employed by the UK company's two main Staff Restaurants and Commercial Services Divisions.

The Staff Restaurants Division is pre-eminent in the UK staff restaurant sector with over 2700 client contracts. In 1994 a total of 257 new contracts were signed with an annual income value exceeding £4.8 million and there were substantial extensions to over 100 contracts with existing clients.

There are also divisions in education services, catering equipment and design services.

The newly created Commercial Services Division co-ordinates the important businesses of the site services company, Kelvin International, the healthcare and defence sector operations, the facilities management company, outdoor and event companies, vending and technical services. Kelvin International is known for its business activity on the North Sea offshore oil market.

From this division, Gardner Merchant Facilities Management was established in 1991 to meet the requirements of existing clients who wanted Gardner Merchant to extend its relationships with them. Services range from providing hotel facilities (cleaning, porterage, reception) to full office and site support services such as security, plant maintenance and estate management. Clients include National Power and the BBC.

Gardner Merchant stress the partnership approach to relationships, their policy of measuring performance with the consumers of their services and open relationships with suppliers. They add, 'There is no short cut to, or economy version of, the people factor in our industry.'

The secret of their success with people lies in their willingness to develop responsibility and devolve decision making power. Their policy is to have small, responsible teams of people who are accountable for their own actions operating within a large, well-supported framework. They say that this structure nurtures, recognises and rewards individual merit more efficiently than any other.

Of their current opportunities Gardner Merchant say, 'The developments that are open to us in the public services sector also present enormous potential provided we can show how enterprise can improve care.'

Range of services

The following list of Gardner Merchant services shows how the company has diversified:

- cleaning (general and specialist)
- porterage
- courier
- building fabric maintenance
- mechanical and electrical maintenance
- catering
- bar management
- vending
- housekeeping
- secretarial
- security
- gardening and landscaping
- snow clearing
- purchasing and procurement
- transport management
- waste disposal
- provision of workwear
- reception
- mail/messenger
- conference administration
- reprographic/office equipment
- archives and storage
- microfilming
- library
- telecom/fax/telex
- car park management
- swimming pool management
- medical/first aid support
- health and safety support
- road cleaning/repair
- temporary accommodation
- space utilisation/planning
- travel administration
- pest control
- asset registration/control
- project planning
- indoor planters/maintenance
- leisure centre management

- crèche management
- general refurbishment
- planned maintenance systems
- structural adaptations
- architectural consultancy
- quantity surveying
- civil/structural manufacturing and engineering (M&E) consultancy
- training centre management.

14 The automotive industry

The attempted Volvo–Renault merger

While it may not seem obvious at first glance, the driving forces behind outsourcing were largely responsible for both the attempt to merge and the ultimate failure of the Volvo–Renault merger.

The merger was to have created a new group of world class status – the Renault–Volvo RVA company – on 1 January 1994. It was to be initially 65 per cent held, directly or indirectly, by the French government and 35 per cent held by AB Volvo, Renault–Volvo. If successful it would have ranked in the top 20 worldwide industrial enterprises, with a staff of over 200 000.

Volvo and Renault had drawn up a document which aimed to regroup all the existing activities of both the Renault group and the Volvo group in the fields of automobiles and industrial vehicles as well as their financial subsidiaries.

The two companies each had their own traits and qualities, developed during a long history, which were to constitute an essential asset in the strategy of the new group. In order to reinforce their roles in each of their own markets, the two brands,

Renault and Volvo, were to retain their own identities, product lines and dealer networks.

One of the most critically important functions to be merged, if not the most important, was the quality management function. This function and procurement were amongst the first to be merged, and indeed were already merged at the point when possible changes of intent were aired in public.

The merger was called off by the Volvo board of directors barely 29 days before its scheduled date. At the same time the Volvo chairman, Pehr G. Gyllen-hammar, who masterminded the project and other board members resigned.

From the time the deal was announced, Swedish managers were unhappy about it. Heated debate turned to rebellion, particularly about the large stake the French government was to hold in the new company which raised the spectre of French ownership. The rebellion was all the more significant because the two partners had already been in an alliance since 1991 and had in place joint operations in purchasing, quality, product planning and exchange of components.

Pierre Jocou had been appointed the CEO of Renault and Volvo Car Quality. Just before the public doubts emerged, Brian Rothery talked with Pierre Jocou about the integration of the two manufacturers' quality systems. In the light of what happened weeks later, the interview, which was published in the Spring 1994 issue of the UK magazine, *Business Strategy*, took on new significance, revealing much about the difficulties involved and the kinds of management needed for such a venture. The interview established that the main technology needed in the merger was management itself.

Before the interview, the following text from a company press release was available: 'In the field of automobiles, the two enterprises have created a common direction called the "Production Projects Plan" which coordinates the strategic production plans of the two enterprises. They have regrouped their purchases in a new direction and created a communal direction for quality. They have accelerated the exchanges of components and put into effect a common platform on which they will assemble Renault and Volvo vehicles. In the industrial vehicle sector, they are engaged in the fields of advanced research studies and the production of components and purchases.

'The joint utilisation of the groups' resources, especially in the fields of research and development, and the best possible coverage of markets, present considerable advantages. It was evident, therefore, that this alliance depended on a complete merger which would permit further combinations of efforts and therefore important savings. Renault and Volvo estimate that the potential savings, which would be much more significant than those which were able to be obtained in the frame of the present alliance, should accumulate to more than 30 million French francs by the year 2000.'

The first paragraph emphasises both purchasing and quality control, and the second the benefits of fuller partnership.

During the interview, which concentrated on the first two divisions to be merged, quality and procurement, Jocou revealed that there were two project leaders for the alliance, one Renault, one Volvo, both reporting to the joint management committee of the alliance. Together with the two company presidents and two managers from each company, there were six altogether on this joint management committee.

He added: 'At the level of merging divisions, my Volvo counterpart and I, both vice presidents of quality, were in charge of the project of merging our divisions. We had seven on our team from both companies.'

Asked what kinds of expertise he was using in the project, his reply was: 'Expertise in human resources. We had to ask what were the values of the managers of each company.'

His response to the question of whether any prior re-engineering was carried out was that there was no need to do any. 'Our job was simply to add Renault to Volvo, and to do it in a nice and open way, not to disturb too much or make big changes, just adding the two together as the first step. After this is complete we will begin to look at productivity improvements, but we will do that in an open manner and with the full knowledge of our resources, capacities and needs.'

And on the matter of the use of consultants for the merger, at each level, division and corporate, the answer was yes at divisional level, and these were human resources consultants, 'including many consultants on the Alliance itself'.

When asked if outsourcing played a part, Jocou's reply was: 'No. There was no new outsourcing.'

Replying to a question about changing or new technology he said: 'The main change in technology was in *management techniques*. These techniques are very interesting and a large part of the job. There are of course new products and new processes, involving technology, but the main problem is management techniques.'

It seemed that the most important issue, almost the *only* issue, was that of people, and the merger was still on at this stage.

Asked for examples of the techniques, he replied, 'Yes, a lean production system, and a lean company system are the main examples. We are also pushing other techniques, values, principles. Such as that the customer is paramount. The emergence of Toyotaism versus Fordism.'

The comments about other benchmarks were revealing: 'We observed everybody. There is no such thing as an ideal company. We might do one thing well, Honda, for example, might do another well. We look, visit, read books, and all these activities provide us with ideas and concepts.'

On the subject of supplier involvement, he revealed that in the procurement division of Renault there had already been trimming, 'very severely reducing suppliers, less and less buying components and more and more buying whole functions. Instead of buying five components and assembling them ourselves, we would ask one supplier to be a leader. Coming back to your outsourcing question, he to a certain extent was also an outsource.'

If, for example, the supplier had been making car seats, he now had to supply the electrical motor for moving the seat, so he had to acquire knowledge of both electrical and electronic matters, which as a seat maker he did not have to have up to now.

In Jocou's words, 'He now has a long-term partnership with us. At Renault, we were already involved in this process and, when we merged with Volvo, we started it there also.'

SCI Systems Inc.

The supplier, SCI, was successful in moving its main business of making electronic components for the ailing computer business to supplying the new electronics needs of the European automotive industry.

During the bad four years in the computer business before 1994 SCI plants in Ireland and Scotland, which had depended almost entirely on supplying components to the major computer OEMs, reduced the share of their output to that industry to half and increased their staff numbers by up to four times.

SCI, a US multinational with a turnover of around $1700 million has 19 plants worldwide, located in the US, Canada, Mexico, Singapore, Thailand, Scotland and Ireland. These are all independent business units in the contract manufacturing business. Although this at first glance seems to suggest competition between the companies, the opposite is the case, as there is a very high degree of resource sharing and even resource switching within the group.

The main reason for SCI's expansion was its successful diversification into such markets as automotive, telecoms, satellite television, point of sale and medical. The most spectacular of these was automotive and their new customers included the French industry.

SCI was not new to providing outsourcing services; indeed, companies such as IBM appeared to be outsourcing even core competencies to them. SCI is involved in design, in the production of prototypes, in pre-production 'ramp' manufacture and even in volume manufacture. While it operates highly flexible cells, some of its lines, such as system assembly, are focused, or dedicated to specific types of products and volumes.

The factors which determine whether cells should be focused or flexible include set up costs and the capital costs of plant. Cells can be focused if set up costs are not high and there is little in the way of expensive capital equipment. On a £1 million surface mount line, however, it is better to be flexible.

The first indications of the potential for diversifying into the automotive industry came in SCI's discovery of the increase in the use of electronic components by European car manufacturers. Although technological change was a good reason for SCI to seek outsourcing possibilities, another important consideration was that OEMs want to manufacture to troughs or plateaus, not peaks.

The automotive industry was going through an important new phase in which electronics were incorporated into its products in what will be a potential $25–30 billion European market for auto electronics by the year 2000. The question of whether to invest in capacity for peak production will lead companies to consider outsourcing to people already making electronic components. There may be 10 to 12 million PCs sold every year in Europe, but there are almost 14 million cars sold each year also and, as Chris White, chief of SCI in Ireland says, 'There is a PC in each car'.

SCI won a contract to produce a range of electronic control units for a large French car component manufacturer. The units include the following:

- headlight leveller (an EU 1995 regulation makes these compulsory)
- car lights left on warning buzzer
- thermo heater for points
- engine management device
- braking systems controller
- air-bag controller.

As SCI put it: 'We got in at a key time, assisted them, told them what we could do, and at what cost, showed them our plant and convinced them that we were a cost effective solution.'

In order to win the contract they hired a French engineer marketing person in France. They identified the companies and the components and went to see the prospective decision makers. They established their own credibility. They demonstrated that the existing SCI products were *structurally similar* and pointed out to the prospects that the market window for new products was narrow, that one way 'to hit the ground running' was to outsource from a plant already building structurally similar products. For example, they would say, 'I know we haven't been building automotive components but look at this, look how similar it is.'

Finally they said, 'We have the skills and the capacity. Why not come over and let us show you.' In this process the workers played a significant role. SCI have a policy that customers can talk directly with the operators. Their skilled and well-educated staff ensure that this is a happy interaction. When the French engineers were in Ireland installing the specialised equipment and wondering if they could entrust it to the local operator to whom they had to explain everything, she replied to them in fluent French.

Ford Motor Co. Ltd

Ford, too, were involved in re-engineering processes as a result of benchmarking. The story is that they were looking for ways of reducing head count in the early 1980s and chose their accounts payable department with over 500 people as a likely candidate, hoping that they could reduce this by 20 per cent.

As they had recently acquired a 25 per cent stake in Mazda Motor Corporation, that company was a convenient benchmark. Apparently, Mazda had an accounts payable department consisting of five people. The difference was too great to attribute it to such factors as size or performance, so Ford had to rethink and reinvent their process. What began as accounts payable ended up with the re-engineering of procurement.

While that was a re-engineering result, Ford also outsources. Its Parts and Service Operations subsidiary recently awarded Computer Sciences (CSC) a five-year contract worth almost £70 million to run its information technology activities in Europe.

According to Nick Bartolini, vice president of Ford PSO, 'The partnership with CSC will enable us to concentrate on our core business of satisfying Ford customers, while increasing the value added through access to new technology.' It could mean 115 Ford people transferring to CSC.

While this was a first for Ford in Europe, CSC already had contracts to run similar business for Ford in the US and Jaguar Cars in the UK.

Nissan Motor Co. Ltd

Nissan's great initial task in Europe was to change the existing adversarial roles of automotive buyer–supplier to partnerships. It also wanted to avoid the European tradition of multisourcing (what has been described as 'just in case') and at the same time achieve security of supply and lowest price through long-term partnerships with a relatively small number of 'first time suppliers'. To Nissan, partnership means working closely together with common objectives of improvement, and having common policies, culture and goals.

The process of selecting partners involved the promise of partnership with Nissan offering assistance with design, productivity and quality. Suppliers were chosen in the end on the basis of quality, cost, delivery abilities, capacity for development and quality of management and the workforce.

Nissan's commitment to this process can be seen in its European Technology Centre which is available to its suppliers who number 200 in the UK alone. The different plants use different suppliers and Nissan is now looking at what Peter Hill calls 'a rationalised base'.

Peter Hill is the purchasing director of Nissan Motor Manufacturing (UK) Ltd and is also responsible for the development of Nissan's European supply base to meet the continuing demand for new models. He puts emphasis on a number of elements in the buyer–supplier interface. The first is the new long-term partnership which has to be based on the credibility of Nissan's declared policies in this matter, as he puts it, 'doing what we said, and practising what we preach'.

The supplier is also expected to have a commitment to continuous improvement and to work to a 'customer quality philosophy'. To establish this, Nissan uses five criteria in its selection process:

1   quality performance
2   cost control
3   supply performance

4   design and development capability
5   management attitude.

Techniques and attitudes of both East and West are revealed in the Nissan supplier interface. They practice joint discussion, open book approach, long term agreements, early involvement in new product development and joint cost reduction. They also *seek to avoid* certain western practices such as confrontation, short-term renegotiation, limited or no disclosure, quote to drawing and multisourcing by price competition.

The Nissan team is called the Supplier Development Team (SDT), also known as the SDT 88 Initiative, and it now has nearly 100 suppliers. The team, using eight engineers, is involved in supplier support from shop floor improvement to training programmes, 'cultural change' and long-term strategic planning.

Pressed further on the nature of the relationships, Peter Hill responded, 'We look at fairly stable relationships as a matter of policy.' This means working together 'on the common objectives of improvement, sharing a common policy, culture and goal.'

On the programme and evolution side, Nissan now has a European Supplier Evaluation System, the supreme expression of which are the Nissan Supplier awards. The system sets defined levels of quality, cost, delivery, development and management performance, which are used also for initial supplier selection. Results are fed back quarterly to supplier senior management, both individually and as a comparison with other suppliers. Peter Hill describes the results as a 'truly lean relationship'.

15 Other sectors

Lucas Industries Plc

Lucas Engineering and Systems Ltd is a wholly owned subsidiary of Lucas Industries Plc and provides an integrated range
of systems engineering and information technology services to
manufacturing industry worldwide. Over the past five years Tom
Spink has been working for Lucas across a range of areas
including business strategy development, organisation design,
manufacturing strategy development and purchasing for businesses both inside and outside of Lucas Industries, and within a
variety of different industries. He is now a Technical Manager
with Lucas Engineering and Systems, managing the Supply
Chain Management Unit. This unit is responsible for supporting
businesses which undertake change projects in the areas of
'strategic make versus buy', purchasing and supplies, logistics
and electronic data interchange.

Tom Spink's starting point is his appreciation of the extent of
the competition facing European manufacturing. He believes that
the Japanese approach is much more than a collection of dis-
associated techniques such as *kanban* (make one, sell one), quick

changeovers (where rapid retooling allows switching of products being manufactured) and quality circles (the Japanese-inspired concept of quality teams). These are mere visible indications of an integrated management approach to all aspects of the business including the suppliers, an approach in turn based on a philosophy or culture of quality and co-operation.

According to Tom Spink a 'strategically selected supply base is fundamental to competitive manufacturing'. This must be supported by systems which are both productive and quality driven.

Lucas spends over half of its total revenues on purchased goods and services and, now in the process of de-integrating to focus on its core businesses, the percentage of outsourced services is rising even further. Recent experience has taught Lucas that a 1 per cent reduction in bought out costs (that is, purchased components) can increase profit by 15 per cent. This reemphasises the importance of the *strategically selected supply base*.

Lucas is one of the few companies to have formalised its approach to sourcing, giving the approach a name – 'the strategic sourcing project' – and developing what Spink calls 'a robust methodology'.

Lucas believes that today's businesses need to analyse their key support systems. They need to match internal systems with the external environment and to understand what makes up the supply side, for example that it is segmented by technology, volume, geography and threat of the substitute of new technology, such as in aerospace the connector industry being undermined by fibre optics. In this complex business, one needs to understand not just the business of one's own direct suppliers, but the businesses that in turn supply basic raw materials to those direct suppliers.

Glaxo Holdings Plc

Peter Garnett, Purchasing Manager at Glaxo, calls the correct relationship a *partnership*. He believes that the arrival of this concept in the customer–supplier alliance reflects the fundamental change in thinking from the old belief that competitive advantage arose from the exploitation of short-term price advantage of some suppliers to the belief that suppliers can participate in the development process.

There is, however, no headlong rush to partnership with Glaxo, as Peter Garnett reminds us that 'there is a significant resource demand in the move towards partnership'. Lowest acquisition cost may still be the general rule rather than partnership.

Peter Garnett uses a system called Purchasing Impact Analysis which categorises the different types of expenditure by the degree of risk to Glaxo profits which could be caused by delivery failure and the value of the purchase. This impact analysis takes into account such key issues as the affect of purchase decisions on strategy, security and other critical elements.

Glaxo has contracted out the running of its information help desk to Prince Training, a small company, because it feels that larger suppliers lack the necessary skills. The deal is worth £500 000 over two years and the small company beat off such powerful competition as Hewlett Packard and an existing provider of services. The need was less for a knowledge of technical matters than an awareness of the 'cultural demands' and, being a training company, Prince apparently had the right skills. As much as 25 per cent of calls to the Glaxo help desk were training-related and not about technical problems.

Prince's sales and marketing manager, Sally Tate, was reported as saying, 'A training company is very well placed to assist and run a help desk. Traditionally these have been run by the techies in large dealerships. That is coming at it from the wrong angle.'

It is not just small companies that are winning outsourcing contracts from Glaxo. British Telecom, through its wholly owned subsidiary Syncordia, has signed up to provide Glaxo with managed private telecommunications services to connect sites in the UK, US and Canada in a two-year multi-million pound contract.

According to Al Albano, Glaxo group telecommunications manager, the company will be relying on the network for all its transatlantic requirements which encompass research applications, financial manufacturing systems, telephony, video conferencing and messaging.

London Life Insurance Group Inc.

London Life Insurance Group Inc. is Canada's largest diversified assurance company with assets of more than $16 billion and revenues of $3.8 billion. Its subsidiary, London Life Insurance Company, is the largest provider of individual assurance in Canada with a market of 15 per cent, twice that of its nearest competition.

The group has diversified and internationalised in recent years. Since 1989 reinsurance has contributed significantly to earnings. A European based reinsurance operation opened in 1992. Another Los Angeles based subsidiary specialises in providing tax advantaged annuities to niche markets. More recently, a Taiwanese joint venture has been set up which reflects the group's development of new sources of earnings from international markets. Geographic targets include the US, Western Europe and the Pacific Rim.

Gordon Cunningham, the president and chief executive, believes that strong national companies have to diversify their geographic markets and that all international companies are dealing with the constraints of slow growth economies and increasing competition. Legislative changes are leading to the emergence of new players crossing once traditional boundaries. 'Many venerable companies will not be among the survivors by the turn of the century,' he says.

Although Gordon Cunningham places downsizing and the need for business process engineering high on his list of survival priorities, he also sees no one solution, but believes that 'if an organisation has a vision of where it is going, success is more likely'. London Life created its own 'for life vision'.

He went on, however, to warn that 'a company cannot be all things, and in the case of London Life we limited our business to financial services, and knew that we had to build good customer relations "for life", that is, from the time they were students until their retirement.'

To help achieve this, the company made a major commitment to a field organisation to initiate and manage the customer interface at the customers' places of business or homes. It was the mission of the company that every day each employee had to do just one thing – meet customer demand.

Gordon Cunningham listed what has been done correctly over the recent successful years:

- The capital base was grown significantly.
- All regulatory requirements were met stringently.

These two allowed the company to:

- be bullet proof
- have capital available
- be able to take on new initiatives.

Next, they delivered what they promised, no matter what the economic environment.

Finally, they reviewed each operation from the points of view of business process re-engineering, efficiency, the competition and each and every business process to see if there was a better way. This review included the prospects for each separate business unit of acceptable long-term returns.

Cunningham lays great stress on recognising and valuing the core business, including the core marketplace. For London Life, despite overseas successes, this is the existing business in Canada, which is traditional retail business not necessarily transferable elsewhere. As he put it, 'We needed to polish, build, nurture our existing core business.'

In the first instance, retail business was not always practical overseas, so they focused US and European efforts on reinsurance and tackled the retail market in Asia through alliances with local companies. Asia was seen to be underinsured, with growing prosperity. It was immediately apparent that the Canadian market expertise could be applied overseas.

The company operates a flat organisation. As Cunningham put it, 'We do not believe that the pyramid corporation with the boss at the top works any more. It is now a partnership, where the employee works his/her own business, with an obligation to provide an individual perspective on the whole company, such as how to organise the work better. No more can we have an "it's not my problem" attitude to overall corporate results.'

Gordon Cunningham lists five lessons that were learned from the successful London Life expansion:

1   A history of success can actually be bad for a company, breeding a fear of failure and fear of what is new or different.
2   Forget the focus on product – focus on customer needs. The 90s demand more services, so the prime focus should be the customer.
3   Understand your core business and what needs to be done for future flexible performance and developments. Adapt your core business to now. Build on it and leverage it.
4   Most companies, small and large, are not in one business but in several. So know your profitability. Do not subsidise one business from another.
5   Never enter a strategic alliance that gives away a strategic advantage. All you achieve is 'short-term gain for long-term pain'.

And finally, on the subject of outsourcing, Gordon Cunningham's view is that every business and department in the company is a separate business unit which has to compete, not just against a possible alternative outsource provider, but for its own survival. This philosophy is also reflected in the UK's Market Testing Programme.

Comparison with a money management company

According to a Canadian money manager, a number of criteria decide what kind of relationship/partner or corporate presence a company has in the different markets. These include language spoken, costs of running an office and the correct answer to the 'why do we want to be here' question.

In Asia, his particular company had alliances with local partners as distinct from London Life's 30 per cent investments in partner companies, which reflect a limit set by local regulations in countries such as Taiwan. Money managers need outsource or alliance partners to do the local investing in Asia. The selection criteria his company uses include track record, size and 'who do you know?' Explaining this, he added, 'Knowledge is a lot of stock, so you talk to someone who knows the prospect.'

He also pointed out that handing over the investment function to locals is outsourcing a core competency.

Cunningham explained how London Life controlled Taiwanese partners in whom they had only a 30 per cent stake: 'We demand business plans, annually reviewed. We don't want him calling the shots'. This, however, raises the question of whether it is possible to have a 30 per cent ownership in a strategic alliance with a Taiwanese company without risking giving away a strategic advantage, and letting that minority partner 'call the shots'?

Barclays Bank Plc

Barclays Bank formed BCO to run one of the largest computer operations in the UK, serving Barclays Bank and other outsourcing customers. Because of their background, their key area of expertise is in managing large, secure, computer centres with multi-vendor equipment and related services such as large print runs of publications requiring banking-related security.

While Bruce Hotter, BCO's managing director, describes the division's external business as relatively small, he believes that BCO will make substantial inroads into other banks, insurance companies, local and central government and the utilities markets. He sees the move towards outsourcing taking off rapidly amongst financial institutions, putting Barclay's new division in a position to attract business. It seems that the entire financial industry is now more focused on cost requirements and outsourcing areas of business it had never considered outsourcing before.

British Petroleum Company Plc

British Petroleum has signed a £6 million, five-year deal with Sema Group Plc to run its international invoicing systems, transferring 12 of its staff. This is the fifth outsourcing contract with Sema.

Reuters Holdings Plc

Even Reuters is handing over work to outsiders. BT has signed a £9 million outsourcing contract for a new flexible bandwidth service which will give Reuters the extra capacity it needs to keep pace with the increasing demand for its global on-line information services.

Aer Lingus

In the summer of 1993, the troubled Irish airline Aer Lingus, which had run up debts of £500 million, placed an advertisement in the international media soliciting a new top executive. The heading of the advertisement was 'Profitability through procurement' and the position to be filled was head of group procurement. In the text was the statement that the ability of the company to compete in the marketplace was critically dependent on the achievement of essential cost reductions. The text went on to mention that the company was establishing a group procurement function which would be responsible for ensuring that value for money was obtained in the goods and services needed to meet the operational requirements of the companies in the Aer Lingus group.

The company had just gone through a traumatic indictment from government and had been compelled to accept forced staff redundancies. With unions already up in arms, the advertisement could not also say in print what else was intended – that any component, activity or service now produced internally, but which could be more productively done elsewhere, would be outsourced.

The background to this situation was that Aer Lingus had been the victim of oversell in the 1960s when IBM sold it a real time seat reservations system. This was supposed to work on two large mainframe model 360 computers on one shift only, so that the second shift could handle all of the airline's other data processing needs. Before the system was up and running, the systems staff found to their consternation that the multi-million pound system did not have enough capacity for what was intended, a far from uncommon outcome for the victims of oversell in the early days of the computer revolution. Instead of announcing the mistake and asking for a few million extra for a third model 360, the staff used 'the great technological breakthrough'. They claimed that they were going into the data processing business and by acquiring a third machine they could sell capacity to other companies.

The step was a resounding success and a spin-off company called CARA emerged. This was in fact offering an outsourcing service in information technology, but it was still called bureau and facilities management at the time. The event, however, was a great internal catalyst that resulted in many other spin-offs such as aircraft leasing, maintenance and hotels. Some of these in turn launched enterprises into the private sector.

The success of these spin-offs was varied. There were also multi-million pound bankruptcies in both the holiday and computer businesses, charges of fraud and the horrendous roller coaster development of GPA, the aircraft leasing venture founded by an ex-Aer Lingus executive, which, within a few years, went from being seen as a spectacular success to being seen as a failure.

Now, after nearly 30 years of selling outsourcing services to others, Aer Lingus, like many another large company, is finding that it has to pass some of its own functions to outside service providers to survive.

16 The Body Shop and the Lane Group

In the context of the Body Shop supply chain, the Lane Group's primary responsibility is to ensure the safe and timely delivery of product from the distribution warehouse into the high street shops. Because the Lane Group delivers directly to the shops, it has the added responsibility of ensuring that the efforts made by the other elements of the supply chain are not wasted by poor service at the final delivery. The Body Shop has demonstrated a high level of trust in handing over this important aspect of the supply chain to a third party contractor, and the Lane Group is motivated to repay that faith with a high standard of service.

The partnership equation

The Lane Group, in describing its relationship with the Body Shop as a partnership, recognises that it requires time and hard work from both the client and itself. While it accepts that there are probably a number of other such relationships in existence which could also be classed as a partnership or an alliance, it believes that this one has been developed beyond mere partnership to what it calls a *winning partnership*. The partnership has developed as a result of following a few simple guidelines, which are referred to as the *partnership equation*.

The success of the relationship is not dependent merely on the managers. There has to be an understanding by everyone involved of what constitutes the expectations, and everyone needs to be enthusiastic in meeting these expectations.

Lane Group management found the first hurdle to be sur-mounted in the quest to reach a winning partnership was the relationship between their drivers and the staff at the Body Shop retail outlets. A demonstration of trust and honesty, reliability and responsiveness between the drivers and the retailers built that foundation block for the successful partnership. As they put it, 'Without a willingness and enthusiasm at the front line, a partner-ship would merely be an empty philosophy which would be prac-tised in theory back in the relative loneliness of the warehouse.'

The Lane Group is a transport and distribution company with particular interests in dedicated contract distribution, shared use distribution and warehousing. It has approximately 300 employees with 280 vehicles and trailers, operates from a number of locations throughout the UK and includes reciprocal business agreements with partners in Northern and Southern Ireland.

Body Shop International Plc manufactures and sells naturally based cosmetics, skin and hair care products. There are currently 1051 shops throughout the world, 239 of which are in the UK and 10 in Southern Ireland.

Within Body Shop International there are the two separate companies: UK Retail & International Retail and Body Shop Supply Company. The retail company supports and directs the retail operation. The supply company is responsible for control of the movement of goods from manufacture through to delivery.

The drivers and the contract team work for two companies and have two bosses. The Body Shop encourages the Lane Group staff to treat the Body Shop as their own company. The Lane Group drivers wear Body Shop uniforms and drive Body Shop liveried trucks.

The partnership between the two groups works well, but why does it work as well as it seems to?

The Partnership Equation has evolved by:

- the Body Shop making their expectations clear – high standards, innovation and honesty
- the Lane Group meeting these standards, being innovative and providing technical expertise
- each company possessing skills in terms of the honesty, promptness and continuity of communication; the importance attached to good communication together with a demonstration of competence has, over a period of time, allowed the partnership to be formed.

Performance standards

A number of Body Shop expectations are set out in the form of performance standards. These cover the perception of the shop staff of the attitude, helpfulness and appearance of Lane Group drivers, their success rate in delivering products at the agreed time, the number of complaints (either Body Shop or public generated), the number of blameworthy vehicle accidents and the cleanliness of the vehicles. The contract is also judged on environmental matters, such as fuel consumption and tyre usage. Some points are measurable by means of questionnaire responses from shops and the monitoring of delivery arrival times on delivery notes; others rely on a subjective assessment by the Body Shop.

Regular review meetings allow both companies to keep abreast of developments and understand the performance levels of the contract. The contract manager and UK distribution manager meet once a week on a semi-formal basis to review performance and agree plans for the coming weeks. The head of operations from the Lane Group reviews the contract performance once a month with the local managers.

The Lane Group's managing director, Rebecca Jenkins, maintains a direct interest in the partnership with at least one visit every three months to review the contract performance.

Drivers are very much part of the Lane Group's success. They are encouraged to make a contribution towards improving the relationship. This is generally achieved through monthly drivers' meetings. These meetings provide an arena for free expression, discussions of expectations, and a review of how they are performing against these expectations. A member of Body Shop staff is present and this enables the drivers to make points to, and get feedback directly from, the customer. The truck drivers are particularly proud of the responses they receive from the shops on the questionnaires. The drivers reflect the values of both the Lane Group and Body Shop in their approach, not only in day-to-day operations, but also in their willingness to use some of their own time to get involved in community projects such as environmental awareness (not necessarily linked to Body Shop or Lane).

Financial arrangements

The financial arrangements between the two companies have also developed over the years and current practice is reflected in the Partnership Document (see page 171).

Variable costs, such as additional drivers and vehicles for peak operation, are directed through the Body Shop purchase ledger. The contract manager is now responsible for controlling costs, but the administration of the accounts is handled by the Body Shop. Previously, the expenditure went through the Lane Group accounts and an administration charge was passed on to the Body Shop. It was to the mutual benefit of both companies to adopt the new system; it saved the Lane Group time and the Body Shop money.

The financial partnership is merely one element of the overall relationship. The relationship is long term and built upon an enthusiasm to achieve an excellent level of service. The two companies perceive the partnership as 'continuing to provide operational and technological innovation and a satisfaction to all involved.'

The authors are grateful to both Body Shop and the Lane Group for providing most of the information in this case study, and their permission to publish the Partnership Document which now follows.

The partnership document

Summary
Lane Group Plc has undertaken distribution to the Body Shop retail outlets in the UK on a formal contractual basis since 1989. The relationship has developed over the years as a result of an open and honest approach to the business.

The Partnership Document came into existence during 1992. At that point, both companies felt that a level of trust had been achieved that would allow the business to operate on the basis of relatively informal agreements. The formal contractual agreement was reduced to a minimum to satisfy necessary legal requirements.

The Partnership Document reflects the day-to-day operation of the contract. It details the management resources, the performance standards, the method of performance review and the broad financial arrangements.

The following is an edited version of the Partnership Document of The Body Shop Supply Company Ltd with Lane Group Plc which includes revisions made in January 1994. In addition to the sections included, the document also includes paragraphs on personnel, performance standards and the contract.

The Lane Commitment
'Our aim is to be the most successful company in our industry. We will achieve this through total dedication to excellence of service. We will provide an international network of services, which offer an effective and efficient logistics solution.

Our core value of environmental awareness and friendly approach will create an atmosphere that ensures satisfaction for our customers and the employees of Lane Group.

Rebecca Jenkins
Group Managing Director'

Communications

Weekly meetings
Colin James and Brian Edgar (of the Body Shop and Lane Group) will have a formal one-hour weekly meeting. A round up of the week's events and forthcoming activities will form the basis of the meeting.

Monthly meetings
There will be monthly meetings with Colin James, Brian Edgar, Peter Smith. The agenda will be:

- European developments
- operational performance
- budget review
- personnel
- technical update.

Quarterly meetings
These will be attended by Colin James, Brian Edgar, Peter Smith and Rebecca Jenkins. The agenda will be:

- review project work
- developments (Body Shop International and Lane Group)
- financial appraisal
- strategy
- performance to date
- environmental.

Minutes will be taken by Lane Group Plc at both meetings and circulated.

Bulletin
The Lane Group Plc will provide The Body Shop Supply Company with the latest ideas and developments in distribution, achieved through a six-monthly bulletin. This will be a combination of updates within the distribution industry, new legislation and technical developments. Off shoot updates are likely to appear. The objective is to keep everyone informed. It will be in an easy to read format, and

further details on any subject could be supplied either at monthly or quarterly meetings.

Strategic vision
The transport industry will undergo significant changes in the next decade. Each year the Lane Group Plc will produce a 'strategic vision', which will be a report on how the industry is developing with emphasis on a global basis.

Driver meetings
Driver meetings will be held once a month to discuss contract performance, company developments and general matters.

Depot visits
Once a month the contract manager will visit contract drivers and depot managers at Lane Group locations in Normanton, Feltham and Birmingham to discuss contract performance, etc.

Environmental targets

Natural Resources		*Achieved/ targeted*
To reduce paper waste	a) Delivery documentation reviewed and paperwork reduced	August 1992
	b) All paper to be used both sides	August 1992
To reduce fuel consumption by 10%	a) BE* to examine impact of 55 mph. BSI drivers asked to observe this as a maximum limit	June 1993
	b) BE has progressed re-route schedule. New vehicles will be limited to 55 mph	August 1993
	c) Quality on the road	June 1993

* Brian Edgar of the Lane Group

Tyre usage	a) BE to establish system of monitoring usage and set targets for reduction. Figures to date indicate an average of 58 000 km for front tyres and 110 000 for rear	June 1993
To maximise use of resources from renewable services	a) BE to question all suppliers and analyse results	June 1993
	b) BE to positively discriminate based on a)	

Waste management

To reduce waste and to ensure all waste is disposed of in a way least damaging to the environment legally and in accordance with our duty of care.	a) Maximise re-use of all materials	Current
	b) BE to identify major waste products and track their disposal route	Current
	c) Drivers Handbook amended	August 1992
To always consider the reconditioning of any item rather than replacing	a) BE to evaluate the relative merits of either option	Current

Environmental Audit

| To be subject to the same environmental reviews or audits as Body Shop's departments | a) D Farrell is a member of the BS7750 working party | Current |

Finance

Open book accounting will be applied to the provision of vehicles and staff used on a permanent basis. These costs will be reported to the Body Shop without margin; a 'x' per cent management charge and 'x' per cent profit margin will be applied. Should the targets outlined previously in this document be achieved, then the profit margin would increase by a maximum of 'x' per cent.

Management fees in relation to the contract manager, deputy manager and driver co-ordinator will be charged at cost.

Each year at a time specified by Body Shop, the Lane Group contract manager and the Body Shop UK distribution manager will agree a budget for levels of expenditure in the following areas:

- expenses and overtime
- driver cover
- overnight parcel despatches
- sub-contract transport
- additional vehicles and drivers for increased volume
- diesel
- miscellaneous items (as agreed with Body Shop).

Where possible, the above expenditure will be directed through the Body Shop purchase system at cost.

The movement of product undertaken by Lane Group on behalf of sections of The Body Shop International, not related to the distribution contract, will be recharged internally by the UK distribution manager. Any profit over 'x' £s in internal recharges will be split 50:50 between the Lane Group and The Body Shop Supply Company Ltd.

17 IBM

The authors are indebted to John Gillett, Director of Procurement Europe, in IBM, for the most frank and forthright account which follows. Here is a company going through huge upheavals of both re-engineering and outsourcing, with all the sensitivities which these entail, and which can still be so informative about these processes that the information about to be given here, like that in the chapter on market testing, can stand on its own, without any other case studies, and be sufficient to convince even the most sceptical that the processes underlying outsourcing are no less than major world responses to the needs of industry and society.

There can be few companies in the world as concerned with outsourcing as IBM, which has been going through mighty upheavals. Like Digital, it is engaged both in seeking outsourced supplies and acting itself as an outsource supplier. IBM is also a huge purchaser, having spent $16 billion in 1993 on production parts, goods and services in its European procurement division, which is headed by John Gillett.

Development of outsourcing

IBM has been involved in partnerships on several fronts including some spectacular alliances with other major OEMs, some of whom are competitors. The big change has been from what John Gillett describes as the former vertically integrated organisation producing most things in-house, from component and semi-conductor manufacture to product design and final assembly, to a new policy of buying rather than making.

John Gillett describes one result of this change as 'having to team up with niche technology leaders, companies who have reached a higher degree of specialisation in particular areas than we have'. A characteristic of these new partnerships is an increasing tendency to share production facilities, and in some cases to share alternate facilities with one partner, say, making one generation of chips while the other works on the next generation.

IBM has also discovered that partners can be used where separate sections of the design phase have to be telescoped into one concurrent process. This has been made possible by devising a common interactive database which all the partners in the design process can contribute to and access.

John Gillett also stresses that partnership involves risks. So much information needs to be given that the supply partner could steal the idea. On the other hand the risks can be balanced with the rewards, such as what he describes as coming up with 'spontaneous suggestions for improvements'. Most of what now follows is from material directly supplied by John Gillett.

During the early 1990s IBM Europe had been transferring a growing number of non-core activities to specialist external suppliers. This trend was reflected in staffing levels, with the company's permanent head count reduced by a third to 60 000 since 1989, its purchases doubling in the period, contract staff reducing and outsourcing increasing from 1000 to 20000 equivalent people – a twenty-fold increase.

Type of activities to be outsourced

Services which have been outsourced range from customer call management and marketing support to education and training, warehousing and property management. From the diversity and scale of these operations the company has gained a broad-based, practical expertise in outsourcing strategy.

At the heart of IBM's approach has been the drive to define the absolute minimum resources and critical 'value-add' skills which are the very core of its business. These are IBM's definition of the core competencies, which fall into the following four categories:

- They provide management and direction.
- They maintain competence and control.
- They differentiate IBM from its competitors.
- They sustain IBM's uniqueness.

Outside these key areas, a huge range of activities existed which are common to most businesses and which have traditionally been carried out in-house. Despite the clear and specific list of core competencies above, IBM found that distinguishing between core and non-core activities was a complex operation requiring a great deal of scrutiny. IBM is aware that in the enthusiasm to divest all but the essentials of a business, there is a danger of losing the 'crown jewels', the features which provide the competitive edge. This amounts to handing over the 'raison d'être' of a company and will create, at a stroke, a potential competitor who could move into, and take over, the market.

Assessing activities for outsourcing

IBM has developed and refined a number of ways of assessing the business for outsourcing decision-making. A simple model ensures that activities are considered as areas of 'responsibility'. This conflicts somewhat with current thinking on 'process management and re-engineering', as critical to successful process re-engineering is the ability to assess processes that cross functional boundaries.

John Gillett expresses this in a diagram which is like a wheel with core activities around the hub and non-core emanating out to the perimeter like slices of cake. The non-core activities include:

- customer support
- sales
- information technology
- property
- human resources
- education and training
- finance
- manufacturing
- development.

This allows both IBM itself and its outsourcing activities to be compared with two benchmarks, known by IBM as 'best-of-breed' competitor, and 'most admired company in any industry'. When using such a model it is important to examine variations and understand and rationalise the reasons, for as IBM puts it, nothing is necessarily good or bad – just different.

Finally, in any comparison of this nature, cost is never what it seems; the true cost of buying services from a supplier are better seen as an iceberg, with the obvious above water-line costs perhaps only the tip. John Gillett demonstrates this iceberg as follows:

Above the water-line
The price

made up of:

- materials
- labour
- overhead
- margin

Below the water line
The true cost of the relationship

made up of:

- warranties
- distribution
- education
- duties
- development
- consignment
- responsiveness

- inventory
- tooling
- premiums
- insurance
- administration
- transportation
- quality levels.

IBM believes that among the activities which can safely be out-sourced are 'critical dependencies', which are important to the smooth running of the business, but not a unique ingredient of the overall product. Even so, specialised management attention is required to safeguard the company's overall capability, and service level agreements must be introduced to ensure that minimum standards are maintained in all the non-core functions.

It finds the argument for oursourcing strongest where significant cost leverage can be achieved, for example by taking advantage of market pressures which are driving costs down in many key areas.

The degree of involvement to be maintained by IBM in the activity being outsourced can vary. A case can be made for handing a process over in its entirety; on the other hand, it considered that as a company it needed to retain expertise in many of these non-core activities. In general this has been achieved by appointing key staff in a liaison role who manage the relationship from within IBM. This nucleus of expertise was considered essential to maintain the company's capability for getting back into the relevant business, should it become necessary.

As the outsourcing strategy developed, it became apparent that the potential of this approach was not limited to labour intensive services alone. It was found that real benefits accrue from outsourcing the complete management and professional structure underpinning a service – and the experience was that the greater the complexity of the operation, the better the yield. The staff involved believe that, had they not taken this approach, they would have achieved only marginal reductions in labour costs.

Building on the success of its existing outsourced operations, IBM is now examining the 'make versus buy' case across the complete range of its activities with a view to further extending this programme. The evaluation process is critical in determining suitable candidates for outsourcing. IBM believes, and this may be fundamental to the success of the venture, that 'it is vital, in the first instance, that there is a "champion" from within the targeted service who believes totally in the case for outsourcing the operation and who is prepared to move with it.'

The people factor

After deciding on suitable operations for outsourcing, teams of people are created from within the organisation to consider the various options from two different standpoints: those staying within the company and buying the service in, and those transferring into the outsourcing partner.

IBM does not understate the people factor, but acknowledges that the social costs of this type of fundamental change in the company's operations form a critical part of the calculation. They are well aware that outsourcing can be perceived by staff as a threat to their job security, and that it is extremely important for a company to understand this and handle the situation sensitively. The financial incentives offered and the level of security built into contracts must be structured to overcome any initial concerns.

Cost savings

Realistically, they expect to break even on their outsourced services in the first year of operation and to achieve at least 20 per cent year-on-year savings thereafter. What they consider much more important, in these early stages, than the cost savings involved are a smooth transition from an in-house to an out-sourced service and the intangible benefits of the new arrangements. Of these, the most significant is the highly focused professional attention to IBM's requirements which is applied by the new service provider and which is often hard to achieve between different departments of the same company.

In assessing the cost/benefit of outsourcing, IBM considers that the full contract term will in most cases be five years. A two- to three-year payback period is unlikely because of the high level of upfront investment required and fluctuations in the business. The 'breakage costs', or the impact of dismantling the economies of scale created under the existing structure, must also be taken into account.

An important factor in the analysis is an assessment of the cost of any contract break or a switch to another supplier, should this prove necessary. In deciding to outsource a service, it is essential to have a plan for such a contingency, which should include details of how the company would re-staff to provide the service itself and what re-entering this business would cost.

At all times, IBM keeps a keen eye on the way competitors are approaching similar issues and learns also from their successes and mistakes.

Another question to be considered is the degree of flexibility the outsourcing option can provide in a very volatile business climate. Cost savings may need to be sacrificed to gain extra flexibility where this creates a business advantage. At the same time, the impact on industrial relations, both within the main company and in the outsourced business, is drawn into the equation when assessing the benefits.

Selling the idea to the board

John Gillett believes that, having completed the assessments and come to the conclusion that there is an unequivocal case for outsourcing, the next hurdle is selling the idea to the board of directors.

In his case, and contrary to his initial expectations, he found that the IBM board's main concern was with the impact on the business, rather than with the potential cost savings. They wanted evidence that outsourcing would improve service levels and that there would be no break in continuity before endorsing the recommendation to move services outside the company.

He found that convincing the board of the longer-term, strategic benefits to be gained was difficult, but was helped by the introduction of an independent consultant who was able to set the proposals in a broader perspective.

In the initial stages of their move into outsourcing, they frequently found themselves sent away by the board to conduct more studies and gather more information to support their arguments. As experienced campaigners, they now arrive to present a case armed with detailed statistics to support every aspect of their proposal and a full analysis of all possible alternatives. While this creates more work, careful preparation of the case guarantees a speedier response and ultimately ensures that the company can gain the benefits of implementing the correct outsourcing solution at the earliest possible opportunity.

In selling to the board John Gillett used the following concepts:

- business impact
- improved service levels
- analysis of alternatives
- independent consultant.

The impact of outsourcing on IBM

The following table illustrates the impact which outsourcing is having on the structure of IBM:

IBM Europe – staffing dynamics

	1989	1994
Employees	100 000	60 000
% purchased	40	70
Contract staff	12 000	5 000
Outsourced services (people)	1 000	20 000

18 Digital Equipment Company

The IT outsourcing market

Digital Equipment Company (or DEC, as it is fondly known in the industry) is a typical but interesting example of a product company wishing to broaden its traditional maintenance and support revenues into areas of higher value and therefore profit. On one side the profits from traditional support were being squeezed by competitors and on the other were the obvious attractions of a growing market. Entry costs are low and new entrants are encouraged by current annual market growth of between 20 and 30 per cent. These growth rates are sustained by the desire of corporations to access specialist, value-added skills which either they do not have internally or which are proving cost-prohibitive to maintain, as the move back to focusing strictly on core business gathers momentum.

The Gartner group of consultants provide the following facts on the IT market:

- At 20–30 per cent annual growth outsourcing is the fastest growth sector of the IT market.

187

- Of the top 500 organisations, 80 per cent will outsource at least one of their IT functions by 1996.
- Of these, 35 per cent will outsource at least one data centre.

These figures are applicable to both the public and private sectors.

Definition of outsourcing

When considering the definition of outsourcing Digital suggests that it is necessary to question both the motives of the outsource seeker and the potential supplier, and to evaluate the various options available. It defines outsourcing as 'the contracting out of one or more business or information systems functions'.

Within administration and finance, Digital is interested in the MIS or IS (information systems) areas which it breaks down into four elements:

1   strategic planning and procurement
2   systems development
3   operations (systems and networks)
4   interactions with the end-user (which could include a help desk and support services).

Of these four, the last three are seen as amenable to outsourcing.
Outsourcing is further defined as:

- long term – two to five years
- a relationship
- a merger of cultures
- joint working
- risk sharing
- strategic motivation
- for mutual benefit.

Risk sharing is included here, even though Digital offers critical information services. However, only by sharing risks can both parties truly share in the potentiality of the partnership.

Benefits to the customer

The key messages which Digital receives from its IT customers about the effects of outsourcing are that they find improved business flexibility and cost savings which are achieved in the following ways:

- reduced operation cost
- increased speed of response
- reduced cost of change
- protection of sunk investment
- avoidance of vendor 'lock in'
- reduced business risk.

Five of these points apply as much to the outsourcing of buildings management, catering, security or any other function as they do to information technology, while vendor 'lock in' is much more likely with IT hardware and software suppliers.

The value added to the service can take place in two main ways: through the efficiencies achieved by better cost management and through increased effectiveness brought about by value enhancement. If a provider can reduce the costs of both the specific service outsourced and its related general corporate costs, such as support at the top, this means that a company has achieved better cost management and thus increased efficiency.

While the cost reduction process is under way, a value enhancement activity may be adding value to the existing business (perhaps by better products and services) and adding value through innovation.

There are at least five fundamental characteristics of the good provided service which are:

1 the provision of the service itself
2 an understanding of the needs of the customer/service environment in which they operate
3 helping the customer to understand what is core business and what is not
4 being flexible

5   understanding where the provider can add value and where
it can not.

Pitfalls versus benefits

The Digital view of pitfalls includes:

- lock-in, no easy escape
- price rises dependent on supplier
- loss of control
- non-performance of the service provider.

As well as the above pitfalls, there are also inhibitors which may
be due to fears, however real, which may stop the outsource
seeker from looking further. These are:

- fear of losing control
- outsourcing being tantamount to admitting failure
- not wanting to be on the 'bleeding edge' (in this case outsourcing)
- seeing outsourcing as a one-way street
- technology developments which may be difficult to include
  such as new work being carried out by key insiders
- contract term which may be too long.

While some may be real, these can be weighted against the
potential benefits, which are:

- cost savings
- better cost control
- improving balance sheet by removal of fixed assets
- ensuring flexible matching of resources to business
- staying in tune with fast evolving technology
- securing access to scarce skills
- enhanced employees' careers
- achieving guaranteed service levels.

Successful partnerships

The successful outsourcing partnership will depend on these characteristics:

- being open
- building a relationship and working together
- knowing where we stand currently in terms of productivity and profitability
- understanding mutual needs
- understanding mutual benefits
- sharing risk.

These are the all important requirements of an outsourcing partner:

- credibility
- commitment
- cultural compatibility
- continuous added value
- contract flexibility
- complementary skills.

APPENDICES

Appendix I   The service level agreement (SLA)

This is an example of the type of outline SLA used in the IT industry.

An SLA is an agreement between the provider of an outsourced service and its principal or customer which quantifies the minimum acceptable service to the latter. Disenchantment will arise from unspecified expectations which are not met by supplier performance.

The object of the supplier should be to maintain adequate capacity and resources to deliver the agreed performance targets for the required volumes. These are some of the main elements of a service level agreement:

Identification of service parameters

- availability
  - weekdays (prime)
  - overnight (non-prime)
  - weekends (non-prime)
  - holidays (non-prime)
- turnaround or delivery times

- deadline achievement
- response times
- security
- meeting the 'service culture'
- meeting set quality levels
- unifying corporate goals of customer and the outsourced function
- committing customer to forecast
- deciding charging rates
- controlling impact on users
- service levels reflecting business objectives and priorities.

Useful quality indicators

- trends analysis, year on year
- measurements of the attainment of the key service level indicators, for example number of objectives not met, number of objectives committed.

Possible elements in the SLA

- mission statement
- business targets
- corporate plan
- business analysis
- systems specification
- service level specification
- services portfolio
- capacity plan
- service level agreements
- personnel policies.

Service level reports

- availablity management
- performance management
- capacity management
- security management

- quality management
- change management
- problem management.

Service levels by service type

- overall targets
- quality
- security
- availability – actual versus target
- capacity/load
  - present
  - forecast
- Reliability
- Performance
  - response by job type.

Set levels of customer satisfaction with

- access
- availability
- response
- change management
- support
- problem solving
- services/products.

Service level development

- performance
  - response
  - turnaround
  - efficiency – capacity
- support
  - quality
  - availability
  - performance.

Making the SLA work

- monitor service levels versus targets
- service review meetings
- customer review meetings
- accountability in supplier job descriptions
- supplier staff appraisal.

Reasons for SLA failure

- not business oriented
- SLA too detailed
- SLA too skimpy
- lack of commitment
  - resources
  - finance
  - monitoring tools
  - support tools
  - management
  - control
  - direction.

Contents of sample service level agreement

1 Introduction
2 Service definition and responsibilities
3 Reporting arrangements
4 Customer responsibilities
5 Procedures for customer/service provider liaison
6 Cost of services

Appendices
A Application services and service levels
B Definitions

Appendix II   A people transition plan

This is an outline plan for both customer and supplier.

Summary

Phase 1   –   Pre-work
          –   Working with customer human resources representative

Phase 2   –   Briefing
          –   Customer responsibilities
          –   Supplier and customer

Phase 3   –   Individual support
          –   Supplier responsibility

Phase 4   –   Offer/Acceptance

Phase 5   –   Induction.

Workforce planning considerations

- skills and experience of current staff
- economics of scale and expertise
- joint agreement of a workforce plan
  - transfer of undertaking
  - plan to move forward
- determine number, types and locations of people required.

Pre-work (not exhaustive)

- statements on terms and conditions of employment
- statements on company benefits
- redundancy liability
- status of existing contracts of employment
- design/implementation of a recruitment process
- design/implementation of a communications plan
- legislative requirements
- planning induction.

Communications

- general communication to all concerned
- management briefing
- group briefing sessions
- individual one-to-one meetings.

Issues

- Major trauma felt by the employees of the company.
- When employees leave, the best leave first.
- If 10 per cent are to be laid off, 90 per cent are unaffected – 100 per cent are worried.
- Irrational, emotional, untrue rumours abound.
- Stress and anxiety lead to lost productivity, absenteeism, accidents and tardiness.
- Political struggles obscure real issues.
- Compensation plans may have different objectives.

- Underfunded pension plans and benefit programmes cause unexpected financial obligations.
- 'Guerrilla Warfare' causes internal rather than external focus.

Positive individual's reaction to change

- What is happening?
- Can I ever cope?
- Let's try and see.
- New reality is dealt with successfully.
- Nothing new after all.
- Forget old ways – they don't work.
- I understand how it works.

Basic questions

- Will I have a job?
- What will the job be?
- Where will it be?
- What will I get paid?
- What about my mortgage?
- Will I have enough money?
- Will I have the same benefits?
- Can I do the job?
- How secure will I be with the new employer?
- Will my performance be adequate for them to keep me?
- Will they want/value me as an employee?
- Will they recognise the contribution I have made?
- Will I have to prove myself again?
- Will they recognise the contribution I can make?
- Will they recognise my training and qualifications?
- Will I fit in/like it/like them/they like me?
- What will my working environment be like?
- Will I have to work a lot harder?
- Will I have a long commute?
- Will I have to relocate?

Possible negative responses

- rejection
- stress
- mistrust
- aggression
- fear
- demotivation
- sickness, sabotage
- timekeeping problems
- isolation
- state of limbo
- attrition.

Useful advice

- quality time with individuals and groups
- talk, listen, communicate
- clear benefits statement
- benefits transition statement
- involvement of partners as group in informal information forum
- clear point of contact for prompt issue discussion/resolution
- statement about job security
- early exposure to new work environment
- quality induction (tailored to each situation) including culture
- provide mentors (cultural and task related)
- regular frequent (monthly? quarterly?) performance feedback
- maintain group identity during transition period.

Employment law

There are three possibilities for existing employees:

1 transfer of the employment to the supplier
2 re-deployment within existing company
3 redundancy.

1   *Transfer of employment*
Transfer of Undertakings Act 1981
If apply:

- all employees transfer
- same terms and conditions of employment, including service
- incoming company takes on redundancy liability
- trade union agreements transfer across
- outgoing company consults
- European Community (Safeguarding of Employees' Rights to Transfer of Undertakings) Regulations 1980
- going concern/recognisable business
- consultation 'in good time'.

2   *Re-deployment*

- Contract of employment
- trial period
- refusal of alternative employment.

3   *Redundancy*

- not a transfer of undertakings
- transfer over as new employees
- redundancy from outgoing company
- no legal obligation to hire
- flexibility on terms and conditions, for example recognition of length of service.

Appendix III Legal aspects of outsourcing

The authors are grateful to Rachel Burnett, of the Computer Law Group, Masons Solicitors, London, for the material in this checklist. Masons have developed a speciality in IT outsourcing contracts (hence the apparent IT bias).

When you are considering drafting, reviewing and/or negotiating the outsourcing contract, the items in the following checklist are the kinds of issues which should be addressed. If they are appropriate in the context of the particular outsourcing transaction, they should be detailed in the terms and conditions of the contract to become binding and enforceable commitments.

Initial decisions
Is a separate non-disclosure agreement with each of the potential suppliers appropriate for reasons of confidentiality during negotiations?

Define what systems and/or services are going to be outsourced.

Confirm the financial viability of the supplier: will the customer require a performance guarantee or specific undertakings about the supplier's insurance cover or an indemnity from the supplier's parent?

Who will initiate the contract draft – supplier or customer?

What resources should be used in drafting and/or negotiating? For example:

- functional management
- technical expertise
- contract management
- in-house legal advice
- external legal advice.

Decide on the commencement date for the contract.

Decide on the transition date for the commencement of the outsourcing services.

What is the duration of the contract to be?

Define the terminology

Define the terms appropriate to this particular outsourcing agreement, for example services and service levels: have the key activities been identified and quantified?

Identify the premises where the services will be carried out.

Identify the equipment which will be used in providing the services.

Identify the software used for the services if information technology is being outsourced.

Structure of contract

Would it be appropriate for any Invitation to Tender and Response to Tender documents to be integrated into the contract, or have matters changed since the documents were drawn up?

Is there to be a single contract or will multiple contracts be more relevant?

The latter may be a practical way of structuring the contract if it can be divided into defined stages, such as outsourcing operational services followed by the development of new services, or if transfer of assets is to be part of the arrangements.

What should the schedules and appendices comprise?

Documentation which is separable from the main body of the contract can be a practical solution to managing information which is very detailed, which is likely to change during the time the contract is in force, or to which certain people need access for operational purposes who may not need to be familiar with the contract terms generally. The service level agreement is often incorporated into the contract as an appendix – or more than one appendix if there are a number of service level agreements.

The following are examples of possible schedules:

- Services
- Employees
- Equipment
- Software
- Fees and Charges.

Staff

Are existing customer staff to be part of the outsourcing arrangements and if so, by secondment, redundancy or transfer?

Do the Transfer of Undertakings (Protection of Employment) Regulations apply?

What is the extent of each party's indemnity in case of any claims relating to employment matters?

Premises

Where is the contract to be carried out – at the supplier's or at the customer's premises?

Are premises to be sold or rented to the supplier, so that a separate property contract will be required? Are a sale, a lease or a licence to occupy to be negotiated?

Equipment/hardware

Is the supplier responsible for providing the equipment for operational running of the services at its own premises?

or Is the supplier to use the customer's equipment at the customer's premises?

or Is the equipment at the customer's premises to be transferred to the supplier at the supplier's premises? If so, is the responsibility defined for ensuring that all consents and licences from any third parties who have a legal interest in the equipment will be obtained?

Is a separate contract necessary to govern the transfer of ownership?

Will a formal valuation be required?

Who will be responsible for insurance?

Who will be responsible for maintenance arrangements and payments? Will a separate contract be required for maintenance?

Software

Will the supplier be using software as part of the outsourcing? If so, is the customer licensing its own software for the supplier to use in the outsourcing?

Have licences been obtained by the supplier for the third party software?

Is the supplier using its own software in supplying the services?

Who will own the rights in any software to be developed in the outsourcing arrangements?

Charges and payment terms

How are the service charges calculated?

Can volumes be predicted and controlled accurately enough for a fixed charge to be viable?

Are charges to be on a time and materials basis?

Is 'open book' accounting an option – supplier's costs plus agreed profit?

Are the charges directly related to service level performance?

What are the charges to include and exclude – are ancillary charges and services separately charged? Are expenses separately charged?

Is there to be a rebate system for breaches of service levels outside agreed criteria?

Will there be any limitations on variations in service levels for the charges payable?

Will there be any development work and how should this be charged?

Do the charges allow for changes in the services?

How frequently may the charges be revised?

Are there any limitations on the criteria for revision, such as retail prices index, computer salaries survey and so on?

Is there any scope for the charges to be decreased over time?

What are the payment methods to be?

Identify the responsibilities of the supplier

For example:

- assist in evaluation of service levels
- comply with service levels
- nominate a representative
- review outsourcing arrangements regularly
- meet customer's standards of security and safety.

Identify the responsibilities of the customer

For example:

- provide information and documentation
- prepare input data
- license its own software
- nominate a representative
- monitor and review outsourcing arrangements regularly.

Assessing performance of the contract

Have realistic service levels been agreed and committed to?

Are there procedures to enable the customer to be kept informed on a regular basis of usage, volumes, trends and so on?

How often should meetings between supplier and customer representatives be held to review progress?

Who will be responsible for producing the agenda, for chairing and for taking minutes at the meetings?

Who should attend the meetings?

What will the escalation procedures be for any problems unresolved from the meetings?

Will there be independent system audit provisions?

Security

Is there a need for confidentiality in the performance of the contract?

If personal data about living individuals who can be identified is being processed electronically as part of the outsourcing arrangements, is the supplier prepared to give a data protection compliance undertaking?

Are there satisfactory contingency arrangements and disaster recovery procedures?

Change control procedures

What are the procedures for requesting variations to the services?

Will the procedures differ according to the type of variation: for maintenance, enhancements or new requirements for the services?

Will the procedures allow for price modification or enhancement as a result of any variation?

Can the supplier refuse to comply with requested changes?

Can the supplier initiate any changes?

Looking ahead: termination or expiry

On expiry of the contract term, should renewal be automatic or must it be re-negotiated?

Should a notice period be permissible following the initial term and if so, how long should it be?

Should a shorter period be possible for termination through material breach?

Should arbitration or Alternative Dispute Resolution be a built-in procedural requirement in the event of a dispute as an alternative to litigation?

Can a termination procedure be reasonably drawn up at the outset?

How will service continuity and transition be achieved in the event of termination?

What should be returned to the customer on termination? Can equipment be transferred? For information systems services, can third party software licences, including the supplier's own licences, be transferred back to the customer or to a new outsourcing supplier?

Appendix IV   Methodology for a company outsourcing appraisal

Outsourcing methodology is essentially the embodiment of good practice in taking management decisions. The decision to outsource needs to be the subject of a proper management process and not simply made, as too many are, on financial or technical grounds.

The methodology includes the simple steps of assessment, planning and execution of a set of decisions.

This is not a recipe for how to go about outsourcing (follow the instructions and you will end up with a guaranteed result), nor is it a black art revealed to one or two privileged practitioners. Indeed, many of the steps advocated are gone through subconsciously by organisations trying to take the decision about what to outsource.

What this methodology will do is help you plan, help you set expectations both within your organisation and outside and indicate those areas where you do need specialist knowledge.

You should look on this methodology, therefore, as a set of tools. In step 0.2 the methodology is customised to meet the needs of the outsourcing project being considered. This is a vital step and usually results in a more relevant overall plan with more directed effort by the project team.

These are the steps in the methodology:

Phase 0 Initiation
Phase 1 Assessment
Phase 2 Planning
Phase 3 Contract
Phase 4 Transition
Phase 5 Management

Figure A.1 shows a schematic of outsourcing methodology.

Summary of phases

For each phase the following will be described:

- *What* the phase does.
- *How long* it should take.
- *Who* is involved.
- What is *delivered*.
- What *decision* is taken.

Phase 0   Project initiation

What it does
Identifies the scope of what is being considered for outsourcing. Sets criteria, initial milestones and go/no go factors for initial decisions. Allocates initial resources to 'seed' the project.

How long?
Two to four weeks.

Who is involved
This phase is initiated by the senior manager or board member who is sponsoring the feasibility study.

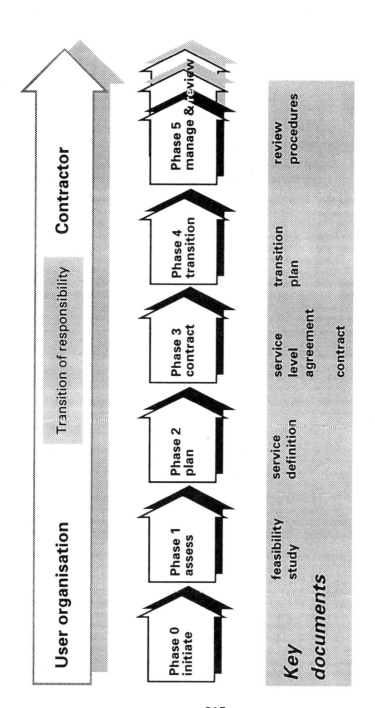

Figure A.1   Schematic of outsourcing methodology
© Oracle Corporation

215

What is delivered
A paper that sets the scope of the project and the management issues.

What is decided
To examine (or not) the strategic benefits.

Phase 1   Assessment

What it does
Examines the feasibility of outsourcing; defines the scope and boundaries of the project and reports on the extent to which the project will meet the criteria laid down.

How long?
Four to six weeks.

Who is involved?
A small team headed by the sponsor, at least one functional manager (e.g. from finance or HR) who is not personally affected by the outcome of the assessment.

What is delivered
Feasibility or other study (see list of contents). A decision on whether or not to proceed to the planning stage.

What is decided
Decision on whether to proceed.

Phase 2   Detailed planning

What it does
Sets criteria for bids, defines requirements in detail and prepares a shortlist for invitations to tender.

How long?
Eight to ten weeks.

Who is involved?

The team set up in Phase 1 plus representation from purchasing (or procurement or contracts) plus legal and HR if not already represented.

What is delivered

A plan for the bidding process including tendering documentation, service descriptions, draft SLAs and a strategy for vendor negotiations.

What is decided?

Who to invite to bid, against what criteria and performance measurements.

Phase 3   Contracting

What it does

Selects a preferred contractor as the result of a tendering process. Identifies a back-up vendor.

How long?

Three to four months.

Who is involved?

The core team from planning phase. Can include external advisers. Will involve potential contractors and their partners.

What is delivered

Invitation to tender. Service level agreements. Heads of agreement. Contracts. Plan for transition of the service to the outsource supplier.

What is decided?

Award of contract. To whom, for what service, for how long, against what measurement criteria.

Phase 4   Transition to new service

What it does
Establishes procedures for the management of the outsourced function. Transfers formal responsibility for operations. Transfers staff and assets as agreed.

How long?
Two to three months.

Who is involved?
Core team, functional management of outsourced function. HR, users, vendor management and staff.

What is delivered
A transition plan. Documented management and review procedures. Handover of formal responsibility to outsource supplier.

What is decided?
Sign off procedures. Date of handover of service.

Phase 5   Management and review

What it does
Reviews contract on regular basis against agreed levels of service. Negotiates to take account of changes and additional requirements.

How long?
One to five years depending on length of contract. Typically between three and five.

Who is involved?
Representative of contractor responsible for service delivery. Representative of user function responsible for management of the contract and of the vendor.

What is delivered
A managed service. Regular reviews. No surprises.

What is decided?
Annual check on validity of original assessment. Decision on continuation of the contract.

Phase 0   Initiate

Step 0.1   The initial management decision

Sub tasks

- what function?
- why (the strategic reasons)?
- what are the expected end results?
  - lower costs
  - more efficiency
  - cannot do in house
- set up working team
  - sponsoring manager
  - functional representative
  - specialists as required.

Step 0.2   The working team

Sub tasks

- set timescales
- communicate with management
- set criteria for decision
- how will we go about it
  (customising the methodology)
- appoint project manager
- set terms of reference.

How do you begin? Checklist of steps
(This is not intended as an extra stage but a possibly useful checklist for all the things which have to be attended to. It contains some of the steps already shown in Step 0.1. A more detailed version appears in Chapter 7.)

1   Getting the commitment
2   Selection of project leader
3   Devising the detailed methodology
4   Drawing up the project plan
5   Creating the project team
6   Implementation of the assessment study
7   Reporting of findings/proposal (if necessary)
8   Selection/planning of the specific outsource project(s)
9   Selecting the providers (including tendering)
10   Passing over control to internal controller.

Step 0.3   The project plan

Sub tasks
● detailed plan of the assessment phase
● roles and responsibilities of the team members
● allocate resources (£££s and people)
● identify external resources needed, e.g. legal, IT, contractual etc.
● identify main activities from the customised methodology.

Commentary
● There are many entry points to this phase but the project needs a sponsor who will see it through the organisation's management processes to a conclusion.
● Communication is a vital part at all stages. Remember, 5 per cent may be affected but 100 per cent will be worried.
● Be clear on timescales at the outset. Do not let a decision be delayed; it is unproductive and distracting.
● Note that the customising of the methodology is carried out in Step 0.1.

Phase 1   Assessment

Step 1.1   Set baseline measures

Sub tasks

- establish levels of service being delivered today
- establish current costs
  - people (permanent, temporary)
  - capital
  - overheads (facilities etc.)
- define tasks carried out by the function today
- map key processes in which the function is involved today.

Step 1.2   Set the scope

Sub tasks

- define the service required
- set desired service levels
- transfer of assets?
- does TUPE apply?
- establish options for structuring
  - in-house bid?
  - buy-out?
- identify target list of suppliers.

Step 1.3   Project assessment

Sub tasks

- what gaps between current and desired levels of service?
- scope for achieving improvements in-house without out-sourcing
- likely influences over next three to five years
  - internal (business change)
  - external (legislative, market)
- analysis of impact on other parts of the organisation.

Step 1.4   Risk assessment

Sub tasks

- identify the main risks
- assess how they will be
  - managed
  - minimised
- assess impact on security and confidentiality practices
- level of risk that will be shared with supplier
- impact and cost of risks.

Step 1.5   Feasibility

Sub tasks

- expected benefits
- likely costs
- risks and how managed
- set plan and timescales for phase 2
- potential suppliers (including role of in-house)
- report to sponsor with business case for preferred option.

Comments

- This step is about establishing a baseline of measurements, looking at the options available and planning a way forward.
- Note that the outcome of this phase can be a decision to improve the in-house function either instead of, or prior to embarking on, an outsourcing project.
- Steps 1.2 and 1.3 can be carried out very effectively in a one-day workshop by the project team members once the inputs from step 1.1 have been assembled.
- Consider involving outside advisers at this stage to act as facilitators or as sounding boards for ideas.

Phase 2   Detailed plan

Step 2.1   Define requirements in detail

Sub tasks

- detailed service description
- inventory of assets being transferred
- performance measures to be applied
- agree what risks will be
  - shared with vendor
  - taken by organisation
  - insured with third party.

Step 2.2   Initial tendering

Sub tasks

- check compliance needs with UK and/or EU regulations
- set timescales for tendering process
- issue request for information (RFI) to identified suppliers
- review responses and agree a shortlist of vendors to receive invitation to tender (ITT)
- appoint external legal adviser if not already done.

Step 2.3   Prepare tendering documentation

Sub tasks

- develop invitation to tender
- agree evaluation criteria
- prepare outline contractual terms and conditions
- define penalties based on risks and assessment carried out in 2.1
- draft a negotiation strategy
  - what is mandatory
  - what is negotiable
  - draft service level agreement.

Comments

- Good preparation in this phase will improve the quality of responses. Too vague a set of requirements will discourage potential bidders (good ones are busy and can decline to bid in 80 per cent of bids). Increase both the price and the price range as different suppliers interpret the ITT in different ways and occupy too much time (both elapsed and actual).
- Do not underestimate the time it will take for this and the contracting processes. Vendors are extremely tenacious. Caveat emptor!
- Make penalties and terms and conditions acceptable in the marketplace.
- Leave room for negotiation.

Phase 3   Contract

Step 3.1   Tendering process

Sub tasks
- issue ITT to shortlist
- respond to vendor queries
- review ITT responses
- supplementary questions to clarify responses
- evaluate against criteria
- use legal checklist (see page 203).

Step 3.2   Evaluation and decision

Sub tasks

- presentations from the top two or three vendors
- take up references
- visit similar sites
- meet proposed partners or major subcontractors
- identify preferred vendor and a back-up if negotiations fail

- obtain internal sign-off
- sign heads of agreement.

Step 3.3   Award of contract

Sub tasks

- Negotiate to final contract
  - terms and conditions
  - penalties
  - timescales
  - transition plan
  - handling changes to volumes
    or requirements
- agree payment terms and schedule
  - one-time
  - on-going
- agree draft service level agreement
- set performance review mechanism.

Comments

- Again, do not underestimate the time that will be needed for this process. The first responses are often not comparable; hence the need to build in a cycle of further questions and responses from the vendors in 3.1.
- The best results emerge from negotiations. Vendors do this every day so make sure you have good negotiating skills. Buy them in if you need to. It is possible that you cannot reach acceptable agreement with your chosen vendor. Identifying a second choice vendor removes the pressure to reach an agreement at any cost with the first choice.

Phase 4   Transition

Step 4.1   Transition planning

Sub tasks

- establish a transition team
- audit assets to be transferred
- detailed plan of transition (people, assets, facilities etc.)
- communication of plan internally
- plan impact on existing supplier contracts
- manage impact on customers
  - consider use of PR
- skills analysis to highlight gaps and retraining needs
- document changed processes (see 1.1)
- consider service delivery/management split.

Step 4.2   Organisation re-engineering

Sub tasks

- train/retrain staff as required
- establish new organisation
- establish detailed review procedures
  - agenda
  - measures
  - escalation
- confirm appointment of service managers (on both sides)
- implement changed processes.

Step 4.3   Transition of the service

Sub tasks

- transfer people
- transfer assets
- transfer service delivery
- implement review process

- closely monitor impact of service on customers
- tune management processes
- transition team handover to day-to-day management team.

Comments

- This phase is about the orderly and planned transition of the service to the new service provider. A key point is not to lose sight of the customers in all of this – after all, it is probably to improve the service to them that was the original rationale for outsourcing. This is a good opportunity to exploit the public relations value of what you are doing. Change is unsettling, and this is implementation of that change so *communicate!* Everyone needs to know what will happen, when, and how they will be affected.
- Take advantage of the change to look at the organisation that is left in house. This is often an opportunity to re-engineer.
- Do not underestimate the new skills that will be needed, particularly service and vendor management.
- Remember the Japanese philosophy in getting it right. Walk slowly to go quickly.

Phase 5   Manage and review

Step 5.1   Regular management

Sub tasks

- hold frequent initial reviews
- regularly review performance against agreed measures
- agree payments and (any) penalties
- implement continuous quality improvement of the processes
- manage changes that are within scope of original contract.

Step 5.2   Periodic reviews as required

Sub tasks

- test service quality with customers
- manage changes in organisations and service management team
- manage changes outside scope of original contract
  - new technology
  - changed business volumes.

Step 5.3   Renewal management

Sub tasks

- carry out (independent) audit of the service including performance, quality and customer satisfaction
- review validity of original feasibility study
- examine alternatives:
  - return to in-house (see 1.4)
  - change vendors (see 2.2)
  - change scope (see 1.1)
  - negotiate continuation (see 3.3).

Comments

- Initial reviews should be frequent but should settle down to somewhere around once per month and should run to a set agenda and be properly minuted and documented.
- Changes are inevitable. Those within the original scope should be handled separately from those outside the scope. Do not confuse the two types and try to manage them in the same way.
- It is in the regular reviews that the vendor management, service management and negotiation skills are key.
- Good relationships *solve* most problems. Hiding behind the contract *causes* most problems.

© Oracle Corporation

Index

Achieving Cost-Efficient Quality
A PARSEC Guide

Graham W Parker

There is no shortage of books on quality. Here at last, though, is one that discusses the subject in the language of business decision-making and is not afraid to look at the financial implications. Dr Parker shows how a quality culture can be combined with a focus on business performance. In a critical and thought-provoking text he explains:

- how to introduce a five-stage quality cost reduction programme
- how to use investment appraisal criteria to prioritize quality initiatives
- how to identify the critical success factors.

The Guide is extensively illustrated with figures, tables and case studies, and contains a valuable set of quality cost checklists as well as a glossary of accounting terms.

Contents
Preface • Quantitative quality • The cost of quality • Macro models • Business economics and finance • Business costs • Price build-up • How quality affects business performance • Defining and classifying quality costs • Cost patterns and policies • Cost data sources • Data collection and feasibility categories • Starting a programme • Presenting the data • Action priorities and economic solutions • Cost reduction targets • Conditions for success • Added value and quality management systems • Summary • Quality cost checklists • Glossary of accounting terms • Appendix: Terms with different meanings • Bibliography.

1995   118 pages   0 566 07582 2

Gower

BS 7750
Implementing the environment management standard and the EC Eco-management scheme

Brian Rothery

In 1992 the British Standards Institution established BS 7750 as a standard for environmental control in the manufacturing and services sectors. BS 7750 allows organizations to demonstrate that they meet health and safety regulations, local and national environmental requirements and the latest industry codes of practice. Compliance with the Standard will give considerable protection against claims under product liability and against unjustified charges of negligence. Both the impending EC Eco-scheme Regulations and a new ISO Standard are expected to reflect the requirements of BS 7750 and buyers – particularly in public procurement – will begin to look for the Standard in prospective suppliers as they already do for ISO 9000.

Brian Rothery's new book is aimed at senior management, including chief executives, quality managers and all managers responsible for operational processes and for transport and distribution procedures. It explains the background to the Standard and provides a practical guide to installing and maintaining the relevant systems, complete with details of certification procedures. It includes specimen documentation and generic models for the registers and the manual specified by the Standard. The system described is designed to meet the requirements of both BS 7750 and the new EC Eco-management scheme.

1993   256 pages   0 566 07392 7

Gower

Comparative Contract Law
England, France, Germany

P D V Marsh

Despite the media emphasis on the 'Single European Market', people who do business across the EC are faced with radical differences between legal systems and philosophies. It is dangerous to make assumptions about another country's law.

Peter Marsh's book reviews and compares the main elements of English, French and German law as they relate to business contracts; especially those relating to the sale of goods and to construction work. He covers

- drawing up contracts
- their validity
- the obligations of the parties
- the position of third parties
- the control of unfair terms
- remedies for non-performance.

As the only single-volume detailed comparative treatment of both French and German contract law in the English language this book will be invaluable to British businesses trading with France and Germany, to lawyers who may be called upon to advise such businesses, and to professionals in the construction industry who may be carrying out work in France or Germany.

1994   392 pages   0 566 09006 6

Gower

Gower Handbook of Project Management
Second Edition

Edited by Dennis Lock

The first edition of this handbook was published in 1987 under the title *Project Management Handbook*. With its uniquely authoritative and comprehensive coverage of the subject, it quickly established itself as the standard work.

For this new edition the text has been revised and updated throughout to reflect recent developments. Eight entirely new chapters have been added dealing with such diverse topics as the impact of the European Community, project investment appraisal and environmental responsibility. More than twenty individuals and organizations have pooled their knowledge and experience to produce a practical treatment which ranges from first principles to some of the most advanced techniques now in use. It is difficult to imagine anyone concerned with industrial or commercial projects who would not profit from a study of this handbook.

Summary of Contents

Part I: Project Management and its Organization • Part II: Contract Administration • Part III Accounting and Finance • Part IV: Planning and Scheduling • Part V: Managing Project Materials • Part VI: Computers in Project Management • Part VII: Managing Progress and Performance.

1994   671 pages   0 566 07391 9

Gower

Gower Handbook of Quality Management
Second Edition

Edited by Dennis Lock

Quality is one of the supreme challenges facing the industrial community worldwide. *Gower Handbook of Quality Management* captures the expertise of more than twenty experienced contributors and covers all important aspects of the subject. The text is presented in a practical, easy-to-read style and supported by numerous illustrations.

This is an extensively revised and expanded version of a successful earlier edition. Among the many new chapters are those which deal with: • benchmarking • BS 5750/ISO 9000 certification • corporate culture • customer service • inspection and testing equipment • materials handling • quality function deployment • total quality management • value engineering.

Dennis Lock has also provided a wealth of suggestions for further reading and a useful list of quality organizations.

Summary of Contents

Part 1 Quality Policy and Concepts • Part 2 Quality Related Costs and Benefits • Part 3 Legislation and Standards • Part 4 Quality Organization and Administration • Part 5 Quality in Design and Engineering • Part 6 Purchasing and Materials Handling • Part 7 Statistical Process Control • Part 8 Quality Functions in Manufacturing • Part 9 Participative Quality Improvement.

1994   832 pages   0 566 07451 6

Gower

The Internal Auditing of Management Systems
A PARSEC Guide

Graham W Parker

This title which is part of the series of PARSEC Guides examines the role of management systems and the corresponding audit process. Dr Parker explains in detail:

- how to plan and implement an effective audit programme
- when an audit is or is not appropriate
- how to develop the skills required
- how to handle uncooperative auditees
- how to deal with discrepancies
- how to use checklists as a tool for auditing
- how to report findings
- how to decide what records to keep.

An unusual feature of the author's approach is the attention he pays to communication skills, including questioning techniques and body language. The text is supported by examples and illustrations throughout, and by appendices of specimen checklists and control procedures.

Contents

The context of internal auditing • The nature of auditing • Roles and responsibilities • The complete auditor • The checklist approach • Dealing with discrepancies • The audit programme • Preparing and conducting the audit • Reporting and following up • Record keeping • The future of auditing • Appendix A Specimen checklists • Appendix B Specimen control procedures • Bibliography.

1995   130 pages   0 566 07584 9

Gower

A Manual for Change

Terry Wilson

Change is now the only constant, as the cliché has it, and organizations who fail to master change are likely to find themselves undone by it.

In this unique manual, Terry Wilson provides the tools for planning and implementing a systematic organizational change programme. The first section enables the user to determine the scope and scale of the programme. Next, a change profile is completed based on twelve key factors. Finally, each of the factors is reviewed in the context of the user's own organization. Questionnaries and exercises are provided throughout and any manager working through these will have not only a clear understanding of the change process but also specific plans ready to put into action.

Derived from the author's experience of working with organizations at every level and in a wide range of industries, the manual will be invaluable to directors, managers, consultants and professional trainers battling to help their organizations survive and flourish in an increasingly turbulent environment.

Contents

Using this manual • Change programme focus: The scale of change • Change process profile: The twelve factors • Factor one Perspectives: Maintaining the overall view • Factor two The change champion: Leading the change • Factor three The nature of change: Identifying the change affecting us • Factor four Unified management vision: Importance of management agreement • Factor five Change of organizational philosophy: Modernizing the organization • Factor six Change phases: Four phases of change • Factor seven The 10/90 rule: Vision and real change • Factor eight Transitional management: Management role and style • Factor nine Teamwork: Importance of teams • Factor ten Changing behaviour: Identifying the critical factors • Factor eleven Expertise and resources: Assessing requirements • Factor twelve Dangers and pitfalls: Planning to avoid difficulties.

1994   191 pages   0 566 07460 5

Gower

The Practice of Empowerment
Making the Most of Human Competence
Dennis C Kinlaw

Organizations are downsizing, re-engineering and restructuring at an ever-increasing rate. The challenge now is to find better and better ways of harnessing the mental resources of the people who remain.

Dr Kinlaw, one of America's leading authorities on management development, sees empowerment as a way of improving organizational performance by making the most competent people the most influential most of the time, and his book provides a comprehensive and detailed model for achieving this objective. Drawing on examples and case studies from successful companies, Dr Kinlaw describes a practical, step-by-step process for introducing or extending empowerment in an organization or any part of an organization, and shows how to use feedback, team development and learning to good effect.

For managers considering, or involved in, empowerment programmes, and for concerned HR and training professionals, this new book represents an important resource for improving organizational performance.

Contents
Preface • Introduction • What empowerment is not • The empowerment process • Managing the empowerment process • The meaning of empowerment • The payoffs of empowerment • Targets for empowerment • Strategies for empowerment • Controls for empowerment • New roles and functions • Putting it all together • References • Index.

1995   192 pages   0 566 07570 9

Gower

Professional Report Writing

Simon Mort

Professional Report Writing is probably the most thorough treatment of this subject available, covering every aspect of an area often taken for granted. The author provides not just helpful analysis but also practical guidance on such topics as:

- deciding the format
- structuring a report
- stylistic pitfalls and how to avoid them
- making the most of illustrations
- ensuring a consistent layout

The theme throughout is fitness for purpose, and the text is enriched by a wide variety of examples drawn from the worlds of business, industry and government. The annotated bibliography includes a review of the leading dictionaries and reference books. Simon Mort's book is destined to become an indispensable reference work for managers, civil servants, local government officers, consultants and professsionals of every kind.

Contents

Types and purposes of reports • Structure: introduction and body • Structure: conclusions and recommendations • Appendices and other attachments • Choosing words • Writing for non-technical readers • Style • Reviewing and editing • Summaries and concise writing • Visual illustrations • Preparing a report • Physical presentation • Appendix I Numbering systems • Appendix II Suggestions for further reading • Appendix III References • Index.

1992   232 pages   0 566 02712 7

Gower